THE WORLD'S

GREATEST

ESCAPE STORIES

THE WORLD'S GREATEST ESCAPE STORIES

EDITED BY
LAMAR UNDERWOOD

LYONS
PRESS

ESSEX
CONNECTICUT

An imprint of Globe Pequot, the trade division of
The Rowman & Littlefield Publishing Group, Inc.
4501 Forbes Blvd., Ste. 200
Lanham, MD 20706
www.rowman.com

Distributed by NATIONAL BOOK NETWORK

British Library Cataloguing in Publication Information Available

Library of Congress Cataloging-in-Publication Data Available

ISBN 978-1-4930-8147-9 (paperback)
ISBN 978-1-4930-8670-2 (epub)

♾™ The paper used in this publication meets the minimum requirements
of American National Standard for Information Sciences—Permanence of
Paper for Printed Library Materials, ANSI/NISO Z39.48-1992.

EDITOR'S NOTE

To help make this book as authentic as possible, in preserving the voices of the authors, the stories here are presented without being copyedited to Americanize spelling, or for misspelling and grammatical errors. For instance, when Winston Churchill spells behavior as "behaviour," we let it stand as written. Also, in certain places, irrelevant and outdated language has been deleted, and paragraph indentations have been added to long, wordy paragraphs.

CONTENTS

INTRODUCTION

BY LAMAR UNDERWOOD

*"How unhappy is that poor man who loses his liberty!
What can the wide world give him in exchange? No
degree of material comfort, no consciousness of correct behaviour, can balance the hateful degradation of
imprisonment. Before I had been an hour in captivity . . .
I resolved to escape."*

These words from the prose of Winston Churchill
describing his captivity in the Boer War of 1899 do
more than launch the chronicle of his escape story. They
instantly tell readers that they have come to the right place
to find vivid accounts promised by this book's title: Escape
Stories.

Whether you are a prisoner of war, a prisoner of
nature's fury, or a prisoner of society, one word smashes
your thoughts against a blockade of desperation: *Escape!*
The stakes are higher than freedom itself—chains

unshackled, steel doors opened, gunfire avoided. At stake is life itself, and the odds against winning the struggle are immense.

The stories in this collection are pulse-pounding accounts of escape attempts of soldiers trapped on battlefields, frontier pioneers on Indian warpaths, and outdoor adventurers facing nature's darkest hours. The pain of wounds, loneliness, and defeat are captured in prose that makes these stories come alive.

In real life, as we all know, escape stories do not always have happy endings. What might have been triumphs turn into tragedies when fate takes a hand. This book follows the same true course, with raw and vivid details holding our attention from the first glimmer of hope to the moments of exhilarating success or devastating failure.

The stories we have here may not always turn out the way you expected, but I'm sure of one thing: You won't be bored.

1

RUN FOR THE TREES!: JOHN COLTER'S AMAZING BLACKFEET ESCAPE

BY LAMAR UNDERWOOD

As a true mountain man in 1808, you are well prepared in the skills and lore needed in the Rocky Mountain wilderness—including the dangers of trapping beaver in the domain of the dreaded Blackfeet Indians. Suddenly, you and a fellow trapper find yourselves surrounded by more Blackfeet than you can count. It's time to drop your rifle or die.

His bare feet were being shredded by cactus that littered the prairie; his gasps for breath were eruptions of blood pouring over his naked body. When he broke stride to look back, his glimpse told him the main body of the Blackfeet Indians chasing him was far behind. But up close, bearing down on him in savage rage, one warrior carrying a spear was almost upon him.

The John Colter the Blackfoot warrior expected to overtake and kill with a spear was no ordinary mountain man, naked and alone on the prairie in late summer, 1808. Had the warrior known that John Colter had been with the Lewis and Clark Expedition to the Pacific, and back, he might have been more cautious. Had he known that Colter had been the first mountain man to explore the Yellowstone region and had trapped and traveled over hundreds of the great Rocky Mountain streams and valleys, he might not have expected an easy kill. Perhaps he would not have taken up the chase at all. But he did not know those things. So when Colter suddenly stopped, turning to face him, the warrior was so surprised that he stumbled and fell, breaking his spear. Colter grabbed the bladed end of the weapon and thrust it into the Indian as hard as he could. The Blackfoot warrior was pinned to the prairie earth.

Now the possibility of survival swept through Colter's mind. The main body of Indians was still coming on strong, but Colter could see the line of trees marking a river. There might be places to hide there. His ruined feet carried his bloody body into new strides.

We know today that John Colter made it to the trees and hid in a brush pile in the river. He survived the desperate hours of the Blackfeet searching for him and a seven-day trek to a fort at the mouth of the Bighorn, digging up edible roots for food. Most historians today believe that Colter was literate. But he kept no diaries or journals—did not write a single word about his adventure-filled life. Everything we know about John Colter, said to be the first mountain man, comes to us from the works of writers and historians—some reliable, others speculating. On today's Internet I counted eleven books about Colter, then stopped counting, turning to Hollywood instead. The movies include three major features about Colter's Run, three or four others have touched on the subject, and some were planned and never made.

Three men actually talked to Colter about his run and wrote stories describing what he had told them. Dr. William H. Thomas wrote a brief 225-word story published in the *Pittsburgh Gazette* on July 13, 1810. Thomas James shared a trapping expedition with Colter in 1810 and penned a much longer version of his story. It is possible that the James story might have some questionable accuracy, since it was not published until his 1846 book, *Three Years Among the Indians and Mexicans*, forty years after he'd been with Colter.

The man most quoted for his account of Colter's Run is John Bradbury, a British naturalist and scientist, who described Colter's escape in his book, *Travels in the Interior of America*, published in 1817.

Bradbury placed the text of his Colter interview in footnotes on consecutive pages about his journey up the Missouri River in 1809, '10, and '11. He had met with President Jefferson at Monticello and knew to expect great discoveries on his journey up the Missouri. Here is the complete Bradbury text, unedited except for the use of paragraphs to break up the narration:

This man came to St. Louis in May, 1810, in a small canoe, from the head waters of the Missouri, a distance of three thousand miles, which he traversed in thirty days. I saw him on his arrival, and received from him an account of his adventures after he had separated from Lewis and Clark's party: one of these, from its singularity, I shall relate.

On the arrival of the party on the head waters of the Missouri, Colter, observing an appearance of abundance of beaver being there, he got permission to remain and hunt for some time, which he did in company with a man of the name of Dixon. Soon after he separated from Dixon, and trapped in company with a hunter named Potts; and aware of the hostility of the Blackfeet Indians, one of whom had been killed by Lewis, they set their traps at night, and took them up early in the morning, remaining concealed during the day.

They were examining their traps early one morning, in a creek about six miles from that branch of the Missouri called Jefferson's Fork, and were ascending in a canoe, when they suddenly heard a great noise, resembling the trampling of animals; but they could not ascertain the fact, as the high perpendicular banks on each side of the river impeded their view. Colter immediately pronounced it to be occasioned by Indians, and advised an instant retreat; but was accused of cowardice by Potts, who insisted that the noise was caused by buffaloes, and they proceeded on.

In a few minutes afterwards their doubts were removed, by a party of Indians making their appearance on both sides of the creek, to the amount of five or six hundred, who beckoned them to come ashore. As retreat was now impossible, Colter turned the head of the canoe to the shore; and at the moment of its touching, an Indian seized the rifle belonging to Potts; but Colter, who is a remarkably strong man, immediately retook it, and handed it to Potts, who remained in the canoe, and on receiving it pushed off into the river. He had scarcely quitted the shore when an arrow was shot at him, and he cried out, "Colter, I am wounded."

Colter remonstrated with him on the folly of attempting to escape, and urged him to come ashore. Instead of complying, he instantly levelled his rifle at an Indian, and shot him dead on the spot. This conduct, situated as he was, may appear to have been an act of madness; but it was doubtless the effect of sudden, but sound reasoning; for if taken alive, he must have expected to be tortured to death, according to their custom. He was instantly pierced with arrows so numerous, that, to use the language of Colter, "he was made a riddle of."

They now seized Colter, stripped him entirely naked, and began to consult on the manner in which he should be put to death. They were first inclined to set him up as a mark to shoot at; but the chief interfered, and seizing him by the shoulder, asked him if he could run fast? Colter, who had been some time amongst the Kee-kat-sa, or Crow Indians, had in a considerable degree acquired the Blackfeet language, and was also well acquainted with Indian customs. He knew that he had now to run for his life, with the dreadful odds of five or six hundred against him, and those armed Indians; therefore cunningly replied that he was a very bad runner, although he was considered by the hunters as remarkably swift.

The chief now commanded the party to remain stationary, and led Colter out on the prairie three or four hundred yards, and released him, bidding him to save himself if he could. At that instant the horrid war whoop sounded in the ears of poor Colter, who, urged with the hope of preserving life, ran with a speed at which he was himself surprised. He proceeded towards the Jefferson Fork [the Madison; he was leaving Jefferson Fork], having to traverse a plain six miles in breadth, abounding with the prickly pear, on which he was every instant treading with his naked feet.

He ran nearly half way across the plain before he ventured to look over his shoulder, when he perceived that the Indians were very much scattered, and that he had gained ground to a considerable distance from the main body; but one Indian, who carried a spear, was much before all the rest, and not more than a hundred yards from him. A faint gleam of hope now cheered the heart of Colter: he derived confidence from the belief that escape was within the bounds of possibility; but that confidence was nearly being fatal to him, for he exerted himself to such a degree, that the blood gushed from his nostrils, and soon almost covered the fore part of his body.

He had now arrived within a mile of the river, when he distinctly heard the appalling sound of footsteps behind him, and every instant expected to feel the spear of his pursuer. Again he turned his head, and saw the Indian not twenty yards from him. Determined if possible to avoid the expected blow, he suddenly stopped, turned round, and spread out his arms. The Indian, surprised by the suddenness of the action, and perhaps at the bloody appearance of Colter, also attempted to stop; but exhausted with running, he fell whilst endeavoring to throw his spear, which stuck in the ground, and broke in his hand. Colter instantly snatched up the pointed part, with which he pinned him to the earth, and then continued his flight.

The foremost of the Indians, on arriving at the place, stopped till others came up to join them, when they set up a hideous yell. Every moment of this time was improved by Colter, who, although fainting and exhausted, succeeded in gaining the skirting of the cotton wood trees, on the borders of the fork, through which he ran, and plunged into the river.

Fortunately for him, a little below this place there was an island, against the upper point of which a raft of drift timber had lodged. He dived under the raft, and after several efforts, got his head above water amongst the trunks of trees, covered over with smaller wood to the depth of several feet. Scarcely had he secured himself, when the Indians arrived on the river, screeching and yelling, as Colter expressed it, "like so many devils." They were frequently on the raft during the day, and were seen through the chinks by Colter, who was congratulating himself on his escape, until the idea arose that they might set the raft on fire. In horrible suspense he remained until night, when hearing no more of the Indians, he dived from under the raft, and swam silently down the river to a considerable distance, when he landed, and travelled all night.

Although happy in having escaped from the Indians, his situation was still dreadful: he was completely naked, under a burning sun; the soles of his feet were entirely filled with the thorns of the prickly pear; he was hungry, and had no means of killing game, although he saw abundance around him, and was at least seven days journey from Lisa's Fort, on the Bighorn branch of the Roche Jaune River. These were circumstances under which almost any man but an American hunter would have despaired. He arrived at the fort in seven days, having subsisted on a root much esteemed by the Indians of the Missouri, *now known by naturalists as Psoralea esculenta [breadroot; Lewis and Clark's "ground potato," an Indian substitute for bread].*

The maze of literature about John Colter—and the fact that he penned not a single word about his adventures—makes the search for the real John Colter and his famous escape rather daunting. The Bradbury account we have here is one of the most trusted. It was used as source material by classic writer Washington Irving in *Astoria* in 1836, and, more recently, by famous novelist A. B. Guthrie Jr. (1901–1991), a Montana-born storyteller without peer known for *The Big Sky* and others.

Guthrie's fictional account of Colter's Run, titled "Mountain Madness," first appeared in the *Saturday Evening Post* in 1947, and was one of the stories in his short story collection, *The Big IT*, published in 1960. A 1961 edition changed the title of the book to that of the Colter story, *Mountain Madness*. In his foreword, Guthrie says his fictional account of Colter's Run is based on the Bradbury story. In it, he dramatically describes how Colter could have used a beaver lodge in his escape. As the *New York Times* described *Mountain Madness*: "Compared to the stylized claptrap of Westerns of book, screen and TV, this book is like a frontier model Colt .45 set alongside a collection of children's cap pistols."

The three interviews with Colter are reproduced in the definitive and scholarly biography of Colter's life by Ron Anglin and Larry E. Morris, *The Mystery of John Colter: The Man Who Discovered the Yellowstone* (2014), available on Amazon.com. Backed up by footnotes for every reference and title used, I highly recommend it for Colter research.

Out of all the varying accounts of Colter's life, these truths emerge as solid facts: After a shaky start with the Lewis and Clark Corps of Discovery in 1803—what was basically a rowdy, drunken spree—he promised to never repeat such episodes. He never did, and he is mentioned in the Lewis and Clark journals for his talents and distinguished service. His hunting and trapping skills made him a valuable companion wherever he went, and he absolutely abstained from bragging or lying. The "Colter's Hell" expression was pinned on him by men who did not believe him when he described the boiling spring and geysers of the Yellowstone region, where he had been the first to visit, and similar terrain in the Shoshone River.

Other Colter solid facts: He was born in 1775 in Virginia; he was a friend of the Crow Indians and tangled with the Blackfeet on more than one occasion; his high-country routes for trapping, exploration, and survival are still debated and traced over maps that may, or may not, be accurate; no Indian arrow or tomahawk was able to kill him; he was married and settled in a frontier home near St. Louis, Missouri, when he died of jaundice in 1813. (At the time, *jaundice* was a common term used to describe ailments caused by many things, including cancer.)

Riddles and puzzles about Colter's life—and, in particular, Colter's Run—still swirl throughout all of the available literature. Was his escape run seven days, or was it much longer? Bradbury says seven; Thomas says nine; James says eleven. Was the hiding place in the river a mere collection of logs, as Bradbury says, or was it a beaver dam, as the other two interviews indicate? The hundreds of Blackfeet Bradbury says captured Colter sounds like a great exaggeration. And what about those maps? Why all the debate?

You could spend a lifetime researching all of this, as several have, and still end up with unanswered questions. It's better, in this writer's humble view, to remember what this outstanding young pioneer did when his Blackfeet captors gave him a chance: He took it, and ran into the pages of something more than mere legend—a very real history of individual courage and determination.

2

CHURCHILL'S BOER WARS ESCAPE

BY WINSTON CHURCHILL

When he published the story of his captivity by Boer forces opposing Britain in the Second Boer War in 1900, Winston Churchill was twenty-six years old. He had already completed duty as an officer with a regiment of the 4th Queen's Own Hussars in Cuba, India, and the Sudan. Although he saw action, it did not bring him the fame and recognition he sought. In 1899, the writing skills he had demonstrated earned him an assignment as a war correspondent for London's Morning Post. *When his train was shelled by Boer soldiers, he became a prisoner of war in a Boer camp in Pretoria. His escape was described in the book* London to Ladysmith via Pretoria *in 1900 and brought Churchill the fame he had longed to achieve. The following excerpt is from that book. Throughout the monumental events of his public life, Churchill continued to produce books, speeches, and magazine and newspaper articles in massive amounts. He was awarded the Nobel Prize for Literature in 1953.*

LOURENÇO MARQUES: DECEMBER 22, 1899

How unhappy is that poor man who loses his liberty! What can the wide world give him in exchange? No degree of material comfort, no consciousness of correct behaviour, can balance the hateful degradation of imprisonment. Before I had been an hour in captivity, as the previous pages evidence, I resolved to escape. Many plans suggested themselves, were examined, and rejected. For a month I thought of nothing else. But the peril and difficulty restrained action. I think that it was the report of the British defeat at Stormberg that clinched the matter. All the news we heard in Pretoria was derived from Boer sources, and was hideously exaggerated and distorted. Every day we read in the 'Volksstem'—probably the most astounding tissue of lies ever presented to the public under the name of a newspaper—of Boer victories and of the huge slaughters and shameful flights of the British. However much one might doubt and discount these tales, they made a deep impression. A month's feeding on such literary garbage weakens the constitution of the mind. We wretched prisoners lost heart. Perhaps Great Britain would not persevere; perhaps Foreign Powers would intervene; perhaps there would be another disgraceful, cowardly peace. At the best the war and our confinement would be prolonged for many months. I do not pretend that impatience at being locked up was not the foundation of my determination; but I should never have screwed up my courage to make the attempt without the earnest desire to do something, however small, to help the British cause. Of course, I am a man of peace. I did not then contemplate becoming an officer of Irregular Horse. But swords are not the only weapons in the world. Something may be done with a pen. So I determined to take all hazards; and, indeed, the affair was one of very great danger and difficulty.

The States Model Schools stand in the midst of a quadrangle, and are surrounded on two sides by an iron grille and on two by a corrugated iron fence about ten feet high. These boundaries offered little obstacle to anyone who possessed the activity of youth, but the fact that they were guarded on the inside by sentries, fifty yards apart, armed with rifle and revolver, made them a well-nigh insuperable barrier. No walls are so hard to pierce as living walls. I thought of the penetrating power of gold, and the sentries were sounded. They were incorruptible. I seek not to deprive them of the credit, but the truth is that the bribery market in the Transvaal has been spoiled by the millionaires. I could not afford with my slender resources to insult them heavily enough. So nothing remained but to break out in spite of them. With another officer who may for the present—since he is still a prisoner—remain nameless, I formed a scheme.

After anxious reflection and continual watching, it was discovered that when the sentries near the offices walked about on their beats they were at certain moments unable to see the top of a few yards of the wall. The electric lights in the middle of the quadrangle brilliantly lighted the whole place but cut off the sentries beyond them from looking at the eastern wall, for from behind the lights all seemed darkness by contrast. The first thing was therefore to pass the two sentries near the offices. It was necessary to hit off the exact moment when both their backs should be turned together. After the wall was scaled we should be in the garden of the villa next door. There our plan came to an end. Everything after this was vague and uncertain. How to get out of the garden, how to pass unnoticed through the streets, how to evade the patrols that surrounded the town, and above all how to cover the two hundred and eighty miles to the Portuguese frontiers, were questions which would arise at a later stage. All attempts to communicate with friends outside had failed. We cherished the hope that with chocolate, a little Kaffir knowledge, and a great deal of luck, we might march the distance in a fortnight, buying mealies at the native kraals and lying hidden by day. But it did not look a very promising prospect.

We determined to try on the night of the 11th of December, making up our minds quite suddenly in the morning, for these things are best done on the spur of the moment. I passed the afternoon in positive terror. Nothing, since my schooldays, has ever disturbed me so much as this. There is something appalling in the idea of stealing secretly off in the night like a guilty thief. The fear of detection has a pang of its own. Besides, we knew quite well that on occasion, even on excuse, the sentries would fire. Fifteen yards is a short range. And beyond the immediate danger lay a prospect of severe hardship and suffering, only faint hopes of success, and the probability at the best of five months in Pretoria Gaol.

The afternoon dragged tediously away. I tried to read Mr. Lecky's 'History of England,' but for the first time in my life that wise writer wearied me. I played chess and was hopelessly beaten. At last it grew dark. At seven o'clock the bell for dinner rang and the officers trooped off. Now was the time. But the sentries gave us no chance. They did not walk about. One of them stood exactly opposite the only practicable part of the wall. We waited for two hours, but the attempt was plainly impossible, and so with a most unsatisfactory feeling of relief to bed.

Tuesday, the 12th! Another day of fear, but fear crystallizing more and more into desperation. Anything was better than further suspense. Night came again. Again the dinner bell sounded. Choosing my opportunity I strolled across the quadrangle and secreted myself in one of the offices. Through a chink I watched the sentries. For half an hour they remained stolid and obstructive. Then all of a sudden one turned and walked up to his comrade and they began to talk. Their backs were turned. Now or never. I darted out of my hiding place and ran to the wall, seized the top with my hands and drew myself up. Twice I let myself down again in sickly hesitation, and then with a third resolve scrambled up. The top was flat. Lying on it I had one parting glimpse of the sentries, still talking, still with their backs turned; but, I repeat, fifteen yards away. Then I lowered myself silently down into the adjoining garden and crouched among the shrubs. I was free. The first step had been taken, and it was irrevocable.

It now remained to await the arrival of my comrade. The bushes of the garden gave a good deal of cover, and in the moonlight their shadows lay black on the ground. Twenty yards away was the house, and I had not been five minutes in hiding before I perceived that it was full of people; the windows revealed brightly lighted rooms, and within I could see figures moving about. This was a fresh complication. We had always thought the house unoccupied. Presently—how long afterwards I do not know, for the ordinary measures of time, hours, minutes, and seconds, are quite meaningless on such occasions—a man came out of the door and walked across the garden in my direction. Scarcely ten yards away he stopped and stood still, looking steadily towards me. I cannot describe the surge of panic which nearly overwhelmed me. I must be discovered. I dared not stir an inch. My heart beat so violently that I felt sick. But amid a tumult of emotion, reason, seated firmly on her throne, whispered, 'Trust to the dark background.' I remained absolutely motionless.

For a long time the man and I remained opposite each other, and every instant I expected him to spring forward. A vague idea crossed my mind that I might silence him. 'Hush, I am a detective. We expect that an officer will break out here to-night. I am waiting to catch him.' Reason—scornful this time—replied: 'Surely a Transvaal detective would speak Dutch. Trust to the shadow.' So I trusted, and after a spell another man came out of the house, lighted a cigar, and both he and the other walked off together. No sooner had they turned than a cat pursued by a dog rushed into the bushes and collided with me. The startled animal uttered a 'miaul' of alarm and darted back again, making a horrible rustling. Both men stopped at once. But it was only the cat, as they doubtless observed, and they passed out of the garden gate into the town.

I looked at my watch. An hour had passed since I climbed the wall. Where was my comrade? Suddenly I heard a voice from within the quadrangle say, quite loud, 'All up.' I crawled back to the wall. Two officers were walking up and down the other side jabbering Latin words, laughing and talking all manner of nonsense—amid which I caught my name. I risked a cough. One of the officers immediately began to chatter alone. The other said slowly and clearly, '. . . cannot get out. The sentry suspects. It's all up. Can you get back again?' But now all my fears fell from me at once. To go back was impossible. I could not hope to climb the wall unnoticed. Fate pointed onwards. Besides, I said to myself, 'Of course, I shall be recaptured, but I will at least have a run for my money.' I said to the officers, 'I shall go on alone.'

Now I was in the right mood for these undertakings—that is to say that, thinking failure almost certain, no odds against success affected me. All risks were less than the certainty. A glance at the plan will show that the rate which led into the road was only a few yards from another sentry. I said to myself, *'Toujours de l'audace'*: put my hat on my head, strode into the middle of the garden, walked past the windows of the house without any attempt at concealment, and so went through the gate and turned to the left. I passed the sentry at less than five yards. Most of them knew me by sight. Whether he looked at me or not I do not know, for I never turned my head. But after walking a hundred yards and hearing no challenge, I knew that the second obstacle had been surmounted. I was at large in Pretoria.

I walked on leisurely through the night humming a tune and choosing the middle of the road. The streets were full of Burghers, but they paid no attention to me. Gradually I reached the suburbs, and on a little bridge I sat down to reflect and consider. I was in the heart of the enemy's country. I knew no one to whom I could apply for succour. Nearly three hundred miles stretched between me and Delagoa Bay. My escape must be known at dawn. Pursuit would be immediate. Yet all exits were barred. The town was picketed, the country was patrolled, the trains were searched, the line was guarded. I had £75 in my pocket and four slabs of chocolate, but the compass and the map which might have guided me, the opium tablets and meat lozenges which should have sustained me, were in my friend's pockets in the States Model Schools. Worst of all, I could not speak a word of Dutch or Kaffir, and how was I to get food or direction?

But when hope had departed, fear had gone as well. I formed a plan. I would find the Delagoa Bay Railway. Without map or compass I must follow that in spite of the pickets. I looked at the stars. Orion shone brightly. Scarcely a year ago he had guided me when lost in the desert to the banks of the Nile. He had given me water. Now he should lead to freedom. I could not endure the want of either.

After walking south for half a mile, I struck the railroad. Was it the line to Delagoa Bay or the Pietersburg branch? If it were the former it should run east. But so far as I could see this line ran northwards. Still, it might be only winding its way out among the hills. I resolved to follow it. The night was delicious. A cool breeze fanned my face and a wild feeling of exhilaration took hold of me. At any rate, I was free, if only for an hour. That was something. The fascination of the adventure grew. Unless the stars in their courses fought for me I could not escape. Where, then, was the need of caution? I marched briskly along the line. Here and there the lights of a picket fire gleamed. Every bridge had its watchers. But I passed them all, making very short detours at the dangerous places, and really taking scarcely any precautions. Perhaps that was the reason I succeeded.

As I walked I extended my plan. I could not march three hundred miles to the frontier. I would board a train in motion and hide under the seats, on the roof, on the couplings—anywhere. What train should I take? The first, of course. After walking for two hours I perceived the signal lights of a station. I left the line, and, circling round it, hid in the ditch by the track about two hundred yards beyond it. I argued that the train would stop at the station and that it would not have got up too much speed by the time it reached me. An hour passed. I began to grow impatient. Suddenly I heard the whistle and the approaching rattle. Then the great yellow head lights of the engine flashed into view. The train waited five minutes at the station and started again with much noise and steaming. I crouched by the track. I rehearsed the act in my mind. I must wait until the engine had passed, otherwise I should be seen. Then I must make a dash for the carriages.

The train started slowly, but gathered speed sooner than I had expected. The flaring lights drew swiftly near. The rattle grew into a roar. The dark mass hung for a second above me. The engine-driver silhouetted against his furnace glow, the black profile of the engine, the clouds of steam rushed past. Then I hurled myself on the trucks, clutched at something, missed, clutched again, missed again, grasped some sort of hand-hold, was swung off my feet—my toes bumping on the line, and with a struggle seated myself on the couplings of the fifth truck from the front of the train. It was a goods train, and the trucks were full of sacks, soft sacks covered with coal dust. I crawled on top and burrowed in among them. In five minutes I was completely buried. The sacks were warm and comfortable. Perhaps the engine-driver had seen me rush up to the train and would give the alarm at the next station: on the other hand, perhaps not. Where was the train going to? Where would it be unloaded? Would it be searched? Was it on the Delagoa Bay line? What should I do in the morning? Ah, never mind that. Sufficient for the day was the luck thereof. Fresh plans for fresh contingencies. I resolved to sleep, nor can I imagine a more pleasing lullaby than the clatter of the train that carries you at twenty miles an hour away from the enemy's capital.

How long I slept I do not know, but I woke up suddenly with all feelings of exhilaration gone, and only the consciousness of oppressive difficulties heavy on me. I must leave the train before daybreak, so that

I could drink at a pool and find some hiding-place while it was still dark. Another night I would board another train. I crawled from my cosy hiding-place among the sacks and sat again on the couplings. The train was running at a fair speed, but I felt it was time to leave it. I took hold of the iron handle at the back of the truck, pulled strongly with my left hand, and sprang. My feet struck the ground in two gigantic strides, and the next instant I was sprawling in the ditch, considerably shaken but unhurt. The train, my faithful ally of the night, hurried on its journey.

It was still dark. I was in the middle of a wide valley, surrounded by low hills, and carpeted with high grass drenched in dew. I searched for water in the nearest gully, and soon found a clear pool. I was very thirsty, but long after I had quenched my thirst I continued to drink, that I might have sufficient for the whole day.

Presently the dawn began to break, and the sky to the east grew yellow and red, slashed across with heavy black clouds. I saw with relief that the railway ran steadily towards the sunrise. I had taken the right line, after all.

Having drunk my fill, I set out for the hills, among which I hoped to find some hiding-place, and as it became broad daylight I entered a small grove of trees which grew on the side of a deep ravine. Here I resolved to wait till dusk. I had one consolation: no one in the world knew where I was—I did not know myself. It was now four o'clock. Fourteen hours lay between me and the night. My impatience to proceed, while I was still strong, doubled their length. At first it was terribly cold, but by degrees the sun gained power, and by ten o'clock the heat was oppressive. My sole companion was a gigantic vulture, who manifested an extravagant interest in my condition, and made hideous and ominous gurglings from time to time. From my lofty position I commanded a view of the whole valley. A little tin-roofed town lay three miles to the westward. Scattered farmsteads, each with a clump of trees, relieved the monotony of the undulating ground.

At the foot of the hill stood a Kaffir kraal, and the figures of its inhabitants dotted the patches of cultivation or surrounded the droves of goats and cows which fed on the pasture. The railway ran through the middle of the valley, and I could watch the passage of the various trains. I counted four passing each way, and from this I drew the conclusion that the same number would run by night. I marked a steep gradient up which they climbed very slowly, and determined at nightfall to make another attempt to board one of these. During the day I ate one slab of chocolate, which, with the heat, produced a violent thirst. The pool was hardly half a mile away, but I dared not leave the shelter of the little wood, for I could see the figures of white men riding or walking occasionally across the valley, and once a Boer came and fired two shots at birds close to my hiding-place. But no one discovered me.

The elation and the excitement of the previous night had burnt away, and a chilling reaction followed. I was very hungry, for I had had no dinner before starting, and chocolate, though it sustains, does not satisfy. I had scarcely slept, but yet my heart beat so fiercely and I was so nervous and perplexed about the future that I could not rest. I thought of all the chances that lay against me; I dreaded and detested more than words can express the prospect of being caught and dragged back to Pretoria. I do not mean that I would rather have died than have been retaken, but I have often feared death for much less. I found no comfort in any of the philosophical ideas which some men parade in their hours of ease and strength and safety. They seemed only fair-weather friends. I realised with awful force that no exercise of my own feeble wit and strength could save me from my enemies, and that without the assistance of that High Power which interferes in the eternal sequence of causes and effects more often than we are always prone to admit, I could never succeed. I prayed long and earnestly for help and guidance. My prayer, as it seems to me, was swiftly and wonderfully answered. I cannot now relate the strange circumstances which followed, and which changed my nearly hopeless position into one of superior advantage. But after the war is over I shall hope to lengthen this account, and so remarkable will the addition be that I cannot believe the reader will complain.

The long day reached its close at last. The western clouds flushed into fire; the shadows of the hills stretched out across the valley. A ponderous Boer waggon, with its long team, crawled slowly along the track towards the town. The Kaffirs collected their herds and drew around their kraal. The daylight died, and soon it was quite dark. Then, and not till then, I set forth, I hurried to the railway line, pausing on my way to drink at a stream of sweet, cold water. I waited for some time at the top of the steep gradient in the hope of catching a train. But none came, and I gradually guessed, and I have since found that I guessed right, that the train I had already travelled in was the only one that ran at night.

At last I resolved to walk on, and make, at any rate, twenty miles of my journey. I walked for about six hours. How far I travelled I do not know, but I do not think that it was very many miles in the direct line. Every bridge was guarded by armed men; every few miles were gangers' huts; at intervals there were stations with villages clustering round them. All the veldt was bathed in the bright rays of the full moon, and to avoid these dangerous places I had to make wide circuits and often to creep along the ground. Leaving the railroad I fell into bogs and swamps, and brushed through high grass dripping with dew, so that I was drenched to the waist. I had been able to take little exercise during my month's imprisonment, and I was soon tired out with walking, as well as from want of food and sleep. I felt very miserable when I looked around and saw here and there the lights of houses, and thought of the warmth and comfort within them, but knew that they only meant danger to me. After six or seven hours of walking I thought it unwise to go further lest I should exhaust myself, so I lay down in a ditch to sleep. I was nearly at the end of my tether. Nevertheless, by the will of God, I was enabled to sustain myself during the next few days, obtaining food at great risk here and there, resting in concealment by day and walking only at night. On the fifth day I was beyond Middelburg, so far as I could tell, for I dared not inquire nor as yet approach the stations near enough to read the names. In a secure hiding-place I waited for a suitable train, knowing that there is a through service between Middelburg and Lourenço Marques.

Meanwhile there had been excitement in the States Model Schools, temporarily converted into a military prison. Early on Wednesday morning—barely twelve hours after I had escaped—my absence was discovered—I think by Dr. Gunning. The alarm was given. Telegrams with my description at great length were despatched along all the railways. Three thousand photographs were printed. A warrant was issued for my immediate arrest. Every train was strictly searched. Everyone was on the watch. The worthy Boshof, who knew my face well, was hurried off to Komati Poort to examine all and sundry people 'with red hair' travelling towards the frontier. The newspapers made so much of the affair that my humble fortunes and my whereabouts were discussed in long columns of print, and even in the crash of the war I became to the Boers a topic all to myself. The rumours in part amused me. It was certain, said the 'Standard and Diggers' News,' that I had escaped disguised as a woman. The next day I was reported captured at Komati Poort dressed as a Transvaal policeman. There was great delight at this, which was only changed to doubt when other telegrams said that I had been arrested at Brugsbank, at Middelburg, and at Bronkerspruit. But the captives proved to be harmless people after all. Finally it was agreed that I had never left Pretoria. I had—it appeared—changed clothes with a waiter, and was now in hiding at the house of some British sympathiser in the capital. On the strength of this all the houses of suspected persons were searched from top to bottom, and these unfortunate people were, I fear, put to a great deal of inconvenience. A special commission was also appointed to investigate 'stringently' (a most hateful adjective in such a connection) the causes 'which had rendered it possible for the War Correspondent of the "Morning Post" to escape.'

The 'Volksstem' noticed as a significant fact that I had recently become a subscriber to the State Library, and had selected Mill's essay 'On Liberty.' It apparently desired to gravely deprecate prisoners having access to such inflammatory literature. The idea will, perhaps, amuse those who have read the work in question.

I find it very difficult in the face of the extraordinary efforts which were made to recapture me, to believe that the Transvaal Government seriously contemplated my release *before* they knew I had escaped them. Yet a telegram was swiftly despatched from Pretoria to all the newspapers, setting forth the terms of a most admirable letter, in which General Joubert explained the grounds which prompted him generously to restore my liberty. I am inclined to think that the Boers hate being beaten even in the smallest things, and always fight on the win, tie, or wrangle principle; but in my case I rejoice I am not beholden to them, and have not thus been disqualified from fighting.

All these things may provoke a smile of indifference, perhaps even of triumph, after the danger is past; but during the days when I was lying up in holes and corners, waiting for a good chance to board a train, the causes that had led to them preyed more than I knew on my nerves. To be an outcast, to be hunted, to lie under a warrant for arrest, to fear every man, to have imprisonment—not necessarily military confinement either—hanging overhead, to fly the light, to doubt the shadows—all these things ate into my soul and have left an impression that will not perhaps be easily effaced.

On the sixth day the chance I had patiently waited for came. I found a convenient train duly labelled to Lourenço Marques standing in a siding. I withdrew to a suitable spot for boarding it—for I dared not make the attempt in the station—and, filling a bottle with water to drink on the way, I prepared for the last stage of my journey.

The truck in which I ensconced myself was laden with great sacks of some soft merchandise, and I found among them holes and crevices by means of which I managed to work my way to the inmost recess. The hard floor was littered with gritty coal dust, and made a most uncomfortable bed. The heat was almost stifling. I was resolved, however, that nothing should lure or compel me from my hiding-place until I reached Portuguese territory. I expected the journey to take thirty-six hours; it dragged out into two and a half days. I hardly dared sleep for fear of snoring.

I dreaded lest the trucks should be searched at Komati Poort, and my anxiety as the train approached this neighbourhood was very great. To prolong it we were shunted on to a siding for eighteen hours either at Komati Poort or the station beyond it. Once indeed they began to search my truck, and I heard the tarpaulin rustle as they pulled at it, but luckily they did not search deep enough, so that, providentially protected, I reached Delagoa Bay at last, and crawled forth from my place of refuge and of punishment, weary, dirty, hungry, but free once more.

Thereafter everything smiled. I found my way to the British Consul, Mr. Ross, who at first mistook me for a fireman off one of the ships in the harbour, but soon welcomed me with enthusiasm. I bought clothes, I washed, I sat down to dinner with a real tablecloth and real glasses; and fortune, determined not to overlook the smallest detail, had arranged that the steamer 'Induna' should leave that very night for Durban. As soon as the news of my arrival spread about the town, I received many offers of assistance from the English residents, and lest any of the Boer agents with whom Lourenço Marques is infested should attempt to recapture me in neutral territory, nearly a dozen gentlemen escorted me to the steamer armed with revolvers. It is from the cabin of this little vessel, as she coasts along the sandy shores of Africa, that I write the concluding lines of this letter, and the reader who may persevere through this hurried account will perhaps understand why I write them with a feeling of triumph, and better than triumph, a feeling of pure joy.

3

STALAG LUFT III: THE IMPOSSIBLE ESCAPE

BY ROBERT BARR SMITH AND
LAURENCE J. YADON

In World War II, bombing German industry with England-based planes was the Allies' only attack option prior to the invasion of Europe. Crews that were forced to bail out over German targets were lucky to survive the experience, only to find themselves in prison camps. Many of these aviators focused on a new objective: Escape!

Stalag Luft III was considered to be an especially important link in the vast chain of German prisoner-of-war camps, if only because of the great number of very important prisoners it held. As the Allied air offensive against Festung Europa gained in strength and intensity, an increasing number of Royal Air Force (RAF) and U.S. Army / Air Force (USAAF) aircrew were forced to bail out or crash-land in German-held territory.

Highly trained aircrew were a precious commodity to the Allies. They took a long time to train—especially the pilots—and, accordingly, the British government put a high price on training them to avoid capture altogether or getting them out of enemy confinement and returned to duty. As early as December of 1939, Great Britain created MI9, an organization dedicated in large part to aiding the escape of airmen from the Germans. In partnership with America's MIS-X, a clandestine organ with similar objectives, MI9's operatives worked as far away from home as China, parachuted into hostile places all over the world, and helped get out as many people as they could. All kinds of people owed their freedom to the men and women of MI9, but aircrew remained very high priority.

By and large, these airmen were a smart and enterprising lot and the most unwilling guests of the Germans; they promptly became a gross pain in the neck for their captors, commonly called "goons" by the prisoner population. A great many of the aircrew ended up at the camp called Stalag Luft III. It was a sprawling installation, close to the Polish border, some hundred miles south of Berlin and near the provincial town of Sagan. The first couple of hundred POWs, British and American, arrived in the spring of 1942 and were confined in a section of Stalag Luft III called the North Compound. The compound was an area almost exactly a quarter-mile square, surrounded by the customary guard towers and two barbed-wire fences. The inside fence carried an electric charge, enough to alert the guards that somebody was fiddling with the fence. The second band of fence was more formidable still, no less than nine feet tall and strung with twenty strands of wire.

As if that were not security enough, there were also coils of barbed wire in the twenty feet or so between the fences, night guards who patrolled the fences, and more guards with unfriendly dogs inside the compound itself. It might have looked escape proof to some peaceful civilians but not to the new residents. Escape planning began almost immediately upon the prisoners' arrival, led by Squadron Leader Roger Bushell, RAF, head of the brand-new escape apparatus, the "X Committee." "Big X," as he was known, was older than most of his fellow prisoners but still a daring man and a born leader. One of the treasured parts of the prewar decor of his former squadron's mess was a road sign he had amputated while landing his aircraft for a drink at a rural pub.

He was surrounded by kindred spirits, mostly young men willing to try anything to escape and get back in the war, or just, as the British put it, to "cock a snook" at the Germans. One of these young firebrands was American-born Major Johnny Dodge, a globe-trotting adventurer who had joined the British forces—first navy, then army—and become a British subject in 1915. He was twice wounded in World War I and won a chestful of decorations, starting with the Distinguished Service Cross. Spending the years between wars adventuring around the world, he ended up in the British Expeditionary Forces (BEF) in France in 1940 and was captured. He was first sent to another camp, where he was magically turned into an RAF officer by a stroke of the commandant's pen and moved to Stalag Luft III.

He was Bushell's kind of man.

So was Jimmy James, an RAF navigator who had walked some fifteen miles with a broken ankle through occupied Holland before Dutch collaborators sold him out to the Germans. There were dozens more, all eager to escape, ready for any scheme that offered even a glimmer of a chance of success. Most of them were already veterans of at least one attempt to escape by the time they reached Stalag Luft III.

Bushell's madcap side didn't detract from his cool judgment; he would serve his fellow prisoners well. Bushell and the X Committee made a couple of intelligent decisions at the outset: First, use of the magic word "tunnel" was verboten for everybody; it was too easy to slip and say it where one of the Germans might hear.

Second, trying to go out over the wire and through the guards and the dogs was obviously a very bad idea; it was plainly not going to work. What chance there was would be to go under the fences, to dig and dig deeply, and that was best done at several points, without putting all their eggs in one basket. Accordingly, the committee decreed that there would be not one but three tunnels, and they would be called simply "Tom," "Dick," and "Harry." (In time, "George" was begun, but that's another tale.) All prisoners would instantly recognize what was meant by the simple name; no German would have a clue. Take "Harry," for example: It was somebody's first name, that was all. And if one tunnel were found by the guard force, or even two of the three, with any luck at all there would still remain a chance for escape.

There were obvious problems. The barracks floors were deliberately built some two feet above the surface of the ground, to give the goons plenty of room to check for tunnel entrances. But you couldn't very well build latrines and showers two feet off the ground, and the Germans had also realized that there had to be some sort of hard foundation for the barracks stoves. So, the brickwork foundations were the starting place. The diggers would use chunks of iron from old stoves, sections of tin can as shovels, and chisels improvised from table knives. And their hands.

For Dick, the starting place was a washroom drain. It was about eighteen inches square and set right in the middle of the floor. The tunnel, however, was started well inside the drain, a block of its concrete carefully chipped out of its side, big enough for a man to crawl through the wall of the drain into the soft earth around it and be about his digging.

A new concrete block to fill the hole was carefully cast from mix German workmen had left behind and had been liberated by prisoners along with all manner of other useful things sent by the X Committee. With the new block in place—the cracks painstakingly filled in with a mixture of soap and dust—and the grill on the washroom floor replaced, Dick was invisible. Similar magic produced Harry, hidden beneath a stove in another barracks block. Tom was started in what was called "a dark corner" of a washroom in still another block.

Which brought the Escape Committee to an even more difficult problem: what to do with the "spoil," the copious amounts of dirt the three tunnels would produce. You couldn't just dump it anyplace, for once the diggers got only slightly below the surface of the soil, the color of the spoil changed dramatically: No longer a nice quiet, unobtrusive dirt-colored dirt, it came up a bright yellow sand. You couldn't just pile the stuff up and hope nobody noticed; it stuck out like a sore thumb in any quantity.

A British pilot named Peter Fanshawe suggested the answer. We must scatter it, he said, scatter it in very small quantities, amounts so tiny they won't be noticed. It would take great care and much organization. It also took equipment, long pockets improvised from pajama bottoms, long underwear, and other trousers. These you carefully filled with spoil, which you then very carefully dribbled away in very small quantities, hanging the bag down your pant leg and walking about trying to look innocent while you pulled gently on a drawstring and bled the bag very slowly of its contents.

Some of the tell-tale yellow sand could be hidden in the little gardens the prisoners were allowed to cultivate. The "dirt-colored" dirt dug out of the gardens could be mixed in with the yellow stuff to dilute it and make it easier to spread. The earth-hiding operation took lots of earth-spreaders, but there was no shortage of men eager to help. They were called "Penguins."

To keep the amount of spoil to a minimum and speed up progress, the tunnels had to be as small as possible, so narrow that only a single man could work at the face at once. Behind him was another man to whom he shoved his gleanings. The second man loaded the dirt into a little wagon with ropes attached to both ends; a tug on the rope signaled another prisoner, who hauled the cart back to the tunnel entry. As the tunnels got longer, there would be even more men engaged in moving dirt back to the tunnel entry.

And the longer the tunnels grew, the harder the work got.

The tunnels were always hot, the air foul, in spite of improvised ventilation in the form of a sort of homemade bellows also produced by the prisoners. And the tunnels were dark, dark as the pits of hell, even with a primitive lighting system, a sort of candle-lamp fueled by fat skimmed from mess-hall soup and from margarine and food fat purloined from the kitchens. A piece of cord made a simple wick. In time, the tunnels would be lit with power bootlegged from the prison system, but until then the dim, stinking, primitive lamplight would have to do.

What to do about possible interference by the guards? Ordinary caution helped, of course, eternal caution in every word and even the simplest action. So did the alarm system inside the tunnels, tin cans filled with a handful of pebbles, actuated by a long string running along the ceiling of the tunnels. At the approach of a guard uncomfortably close to the tunnel entry, a little tug on the string brought strict silence. Other prisoners formed a surveillance system, keeping track of where the goons were and where they were probably going.

The diggers had to be endlessly vigilant about their everyday prison clothing as well. No trace of the tell-tale yellow sand could be allowed outside where guard personnel might see it, either piled on the ground or smeared on a digger's clothing. Accordingly, everybody in the tunnels worked either naked or in long johns.

Tunnel Tom was a good illustration of the system in action. The spoil came back down the tunnel and up to the washroom in cans. These were dumped on the floor on a blanket tended by American Tom Minskewitz, who filled the trouser-leg bags of the Penguins. They then went about their casual strolling, their gardening, or their group masquerades. The blanket kept the washroom floor clear of the deadly yellow sand while the distributors' bags were filled.

The dirt distribution systems were many and varied. American Jerry Sage, for example, had organized a sort of drill team—forty men or so—as a means of exercise and passing the time. These men practiced their drills assiduously with ten or twelve earth-scatterers marching in the middle of their formation. Some of the spectators at prisoner volleyball games also left a little yellow sand behind them. The system worked.

For a while, at least. And then a prisoner got careless, a Penguin who unloaded too much of his bag of yellow sand in one place while standing alone a little distance away from the crowd at a volleyball match. Before anybody could pick it up or scatter it, it was spotted by a guard. The goons now knew that there was digging underway someplace.

An orgy of searching found nothing, however; the Germans even drove trucks up and down in the compound, obviously intending to cave in any tunnels; they could not know that Tom, Dick, and Harry were thirty feet below them. The goons even went so far as to hide a couple of their men in the ceiling of one prison block, presumably to eavesdrop on prisoners' guilty language. There were almost daily barracks searches.

Then came the Germans' maximum effort: an incursion by about a hundred soldiers, who industriously dug a four-foot-deep ditch across the compound and then began poking steel rods down its bottom, obviously probing for the roof of any tunnel. There was some excitement among the searchers when one probe hit something hard. Their prize turned out to be a rock, to the intense amusement of their prisoner audience.

The guards got nothing except acute embarrassment, but the need for increased caution was obvious to the diggers, and the work slowed dramatically. One solution was to stop work on Tunnel Dick and turn it into a dump for the treacherous sand. Abandoning Dick had another advantage: now, a few pieces at a time, the diggers could also remove and reuse Dick's timbering, the mattress slats from the beds of a good many prisoners. The slats, some four thousand of them, were only part of the colossal infusion of German property converted by the prisoners to serve the Allied war effort. Included were hundreds of pieces of eating utensils, over a thousand feet of rope, hundreds of blankets and towels, and some 1,400 tin cans.

Probably the most important loot were two large rolls of electrical wire. These had been left on the ground by a German electrician while he perched on a ladder wiring something else and were casually picked up and boldly liberated by a passing member of the escape team. The two rolls became the heart of the tunnel lighting system; no longer were the diggers required to grope about in primordial gloom and the stench of smoldering grease. The run of good luck was interrupted by a sad event: the transfer of the American prisoners to another camp not long before the projected time of the tunnels' completion. The Yanks, as the British called them, had contributed much to what would later become known as the Great Escape; now they could not share in it. If their transfer was a profound disappointment at the time, time would reveal it as a mixed blessing.

The work went on until Tom was making as much as ten feet a day; it was almost into the woods surrounding the compound, and then the blow fell; the Germans sent a work party out to cut down trees and brush until the shelter of the woods had been pushed back a hundred feet or so.

Worse was to come.

A surprise search discovered the entrance to Tom. While a guard was painstakingly tapping one of the washroom floors, his little metal rod lodged in a minute crack. He pushed on with his careful inquiry, more guards pitched in, and the result was the discovery and destruction of Tom. A guard who crawled to the end and back is said have taken a half-hour for the round trip. It was a blow, after all the sweat and the filth, the danger and the sacrifice, but Bushell cast it in the right light. "We're going ahead," he said, and added, "we still have two tunnels; the Germans probably think we don't have any." And so, although the Escape Committee suspended digging operations for a while, mostly because of bitter cold weather, they started again in earnest when the new year arrived.

Harry now advanced as many as ten or twelve feet a day, until it reached almost 350 feet. Since the distance to the forest was estimated at 335 feet, it was at last time to dig another direction . . . up. This time there would be no last-minute disappointment, for the initial upward dig hit what the prisoners had long hoped for: tree roots. And at last, in March, a metal rod pushed into the roof of the upward leg of the tunnel broke through with only six inches to go to the surface.

Freedom was just half a foot away.

Last-minute planning also called for two things: the best weather possible at this time of year and, if possible, a moonless night. The Escape Committee settled on March 24. While the digging had been going on, the forgers had been busy with all kinds of false documents, identity cards, and passes and paybooks and such, of which there seemed to be an endless variety. Nobody traveled in Nazi Europe without at least one such *ausweis*, generally more. Nobody could. Whatever disguise each escaper chose, his paper had to match; it had to have a convincing picture and the appropriate date stamp, and it had to appear wrinkled and a little faded with use.

Some of the forgers' raw materials came from goons hungry for decent cigarettes and other treasures from Red Cross parcels. Trading was done on the barter system, of which the unit of measurement was the cigarette. Some required documents were improvised on the spot; for instance, quite useful official-looking stamps—without which no German document was complete—were created from boot soles. The necessary ID photographs were taken with a German officer's borrowed Leica, ostensibly for mailing home.

RAF flight lieutenant Tim Walenn had been a graphic artist as a civilian; he became forger-in-chief, responsible for producing the enormous quantity of paper. The men due to escape had chosen their identities and the costumes that matched them. They had necessarily also chosen their nationality. All the documents Walenn and his forgery crew produced had to match an escaper . . . and be both convincing and current.

Some prisoners spoke fluent French or German; some were native speakers of other tongues, like Polish and Dutch. Some British officers could manage no language save their own, at least not convincingly. These men chose identities that required a speech few Germans were likely to understand. Bulgarian was popular; one prisoner put it pretty well: "Nobody speaks Bulgarian except the Bulgarians, and they're 600 miles away"—which had a certain logic to it, although the Escape Committee turned that man down. At least two others did go out as Bulgarians, "forestry students"; that guise would at least give them a chance of accounting for themselves if the Germans caught them skulking about in the woods.

These men were part of the contingent called "hard-assers," men planning to make their escape cross-country, hiding where they could, living rough, traveling fast in what promised to be vile weather. At least the hard-assers didn't have to worry as much about inquisitive waiters and desk clerks, busybody train conductors, and nosy policemen.

The underground tailor shop also had much painstaking work to do before the break. Staffed mostly by Czech and Polish officers, the tailors turned out everything from business suits to German military uniforms to foreign workers' dungarees. Their work took immense care; you might get away with converting a military tunic to a civilian coat if you were very, very careful, but you had to pay the closest attention to every detail, even little things like buttons and stripes.

Compasses for the hard-assers were created by painstakingly magnetizing prisoners' razor blades, then breaking them into tiny slivers. Compass cases came from melted plastic phonograph records, and luminous compass points were created from the hands of the commandant's own alarm clock, purloined from his office. The genius who made these useful things was an Australian named Hake, whose finishing touch was stamping each of his compasses "Made in Stalag Luft III. Patent Pending." By the spring of 1944, he had turned out more than five hundred compasses.

Nobody would go out armed. Even had they been able to obtain weaponry, it would have done them little good in the middle of Fortress Europe. It would simply have gotten them killed, shot down during arrest, or murdered by the Gestapo later. Wits and careful preparation were the prisoners' weapons; they carried nothing more deadly than their prisoner dog tags, essential to any kind of decent treatment if they were recaptured.

Some elected to travel alone. Others went out in pairs or even slightly larger groups. There was some comfort in not being alone, and two or more prisoners could help each other. But large groups of prisoners were almost sure to attract more unwelcome attention than a man alone or a companionable pair.

Then came the hard part: How many prisoners could try the break, and how would they be selected? The committee made the tough calls, since the best estimates were that a total of no more than 200 to 220 POWs could make it through the tunnel in a single night, and more than 500 men wanted to go. The first thirty were chosen as having the best chance for escape, because of some special quality, such as fluency in French or other languages. They would all travel by train, and the early start would help guarantee them time to get to the local railroad station in time to have their pick of trains.

Bushell and his committee would then hold a drawing for the remaining spaces, and these men would go out in the order in which their names had been drawn. The next twenty spaces were chosen from those who had worked hardest in the tunnel; ten more from the biggest contributors among the forgers and tailors and gadget-makers and Penguins. The rest of the 200 or so were chosen in a blind draw from everybody else who wanted to go. There was much disappointment.

At zero hour, the first seventeen men were poised at the head of the tunnel, waiting for it to be opened into the darkness and cool of the woods . . . and freedom. It was only then that they made the saddest discovery of all their days in the prison camps. The diggers' calculations had been in error . . . the shelter of the woods was still some ten feet away. And about forty short feet away to one side of the tunnel exit, in plain view, there was a sentry post, and it was manned.

Bushell had an enormous command decision to make, and just minutes to make it.

We go, he said; we can't wait another month. The risk in waiting for another favorable moon was too great. Every day of delay heightened the chance of a guard or an informant learning something, of a prisoner slipping. And now they had the exit hole to worry about.

And so the file of POWs traveled one by one down the long tunnel on the little trolley that had served to evacuate all that spoil, carefully holding their baggage out in front of them—the size and weight of what each man would carry had already been passed on by the Escape Committee.

At one point the electric lighting shut down for a half hour or so, courtesy of the Royal Air Force; some eight hundred British bombers were on their way to Berlin. The German capital was a hundred or so miles away, but the Germans regularly turned off the power of any city or town that might furnish a landmark to guide Allied aircraft to Berlin. If the shutdown pitched the tunnel into stygian gloom, it also extinguished the camp's exterior lighting, including the searchlights along the perimeter fence. That at least was some help to the escapers who had already reached the tunnel exit.

The exit itself was the first obstacle. The tunnel hatch was frozen shut in this miserably cold weather, and it took more than an hour in the gloom of the exit tunnel to break it loose. Some of the baggage also caused problems, falling off or momentarily jamming the progress of the little trolley. It was much worse for RAF officer Tom Kirby-Green: his suitcase hung up on some of the tunnel's timbering and he was buried in a cave-in deep in the pitch-black tunnel. Frantic digging by the other prisoners got him out shaken and unhurt, but the process took the better part of an hour. More delay.

And so, after all the toil and worry, the sweat and the planning and the careful precautions, the rest of the escapers would not get to breathe free air after all. It was a bitter pill. Those who hadn't made it out hastily burned their false papers—"dozens of little bonfires" as one source put it—while others feasted hastily on their carefully hoarded bits of traveling food.

In the end, after a series of wild adventures, only three men finally reached safety, just three of the dozens who started out. Two were Norwegian officers, the third a Dutchman; all of them were intimately familiar with Europe, fluent in other languages. None of the hardassers made it; the bitter weather and deep snow made off-road travel impossible.

On the plus side, however, those who made it out and survived tasted a priceless bit of freedom and gave fits to the German jailers and hunters. One RAF man, Jimmy James, put it pretty well: "I climbed up the ladder and the first thing I saw were stars. I thought of the RAF motto—*Per Ardua ad Astra* (through adversity to the stars). . . . I lost some good friends in that escape . . . some of the finest men I've ever known." Jimmy would survive the war, in spite of being part of no fewer than a dozen escape attempts.

Seventeen of the recaptured escapers were returned to Stalag Luft III. Four more were sent to the concentration camp at Sachsenhausen, near Frankfurt. All four dug their way out and won a few weeks more of freedom, only to be recaptured and returned to Sachsenhausen camp. Two more ended up in the maximum security of Colditz Castle.

Sadly, inexcusably, foully, some fifty were executed after capture, killings that were premeditated murder in the simplest sense. Hitler had initially decreed that all recaptured officers were to be executed, and only reduced the number slightly after pleas from several high-ranking officers—among them Goering and Field-Marshal Keitel—that such killings plainly violated the Geneva Conventions.

Since early 1944, the protection of the Geneva Conventions had been increasingly ignored by the German authority, in particular the Gestapo. Muller, the Gestapo chief, ordered (in secret, of course) that all recaptured escapers, except British and Americans, were to be taken to Mauthausen concentration camp and shot out of hand. This order was appropriately called *Aktion Kugel*, the "Bullet Decree."

Among the dead was Big X, Roger Bushell. Bushell was shot along with a fellow officer near Saarbrueken, Germany, by a pair of Gestapo men. Bushell and his companion had made some eight hundred miles in about ten hours by fast train. When their luck ran out, the two officers were only two hours from France, where they stood a good chance of getting help from the Resistance.

The man who killed Big X, Emil Schulz, survived the war. He did not, however, survive British justice. The second Gestapo murderer was killed before the fighting ended.

Jimmy James made it through the war, along with thousands of other inmates of Sachsenhausen. The commandant got a Himmler *Befehl* (directive, order) on the first of February 1945, directing the extermination of the entire prisoner population, but the British contingent survived courtesy of a friendly police inspector. The prisoners ended up in a comparative paradise, a town in the peaceful Dolomite Alps.

For most of the escapers, at least, the whole exercise had been well worth it, in spite of the hardship and danger and disappointment, in spite of the grief the murder of their comrades caused them. Spitfire pilot Sidney Dowse, already a veteran escaper before he left Harry behind him, put it this way: "We caused havoc to the Germans and tied up thousands if not millions of them in the search for us."

Another Spitfire pilot, New Zealander Mike Shand, said much the same thing: "It was worth it. I don't think any of us thought we'd make it back to England . . . but we had to do something. We did it to cause chaos behind enemy lines and that's exactly what we did."

The end of captivity for Johnny Dodge was not only miraculous but bizarre. Pulled out of confinement by an SS officer, he was whisked off to Berlin, dressed in civilian clothes, housed in the ritzy Adlon Hotel, and wined and dined. The reason soon became clear. He was to carry a peace proposal to England and present it to his "kinsman," none other than Winston Churchill (they were not, in fact, related). The German offer itself served to demonstrate the surreal, phantom world that was Berlin at the end of the war: Hitler would settle for nothing less than a British guarantee that Germany's prewar boundaries would be maintained. At the end of Dodge's long trip home, he did get to see Churchill, who entertained him at 10 Downing Street. Two days later, Germany surrendered unconditionally.

It seems appropriate to close with something St. Matthew wrote a very long time ago. It is a short writing only, and already appears in a couple of excellent books on the "great escape." That does not lessen its power a bit, and I shamelessly quote it again here, for what St. Matthew said fits precisely the spirit that moved and sustained the men of Stalag Luft III, the men who would not give up: "And fear not them that kill the body, and are not able to kill the soul." No matter how tough things got, no matter how dangerous, the souls of the men of Stalag Luft III never wavered.

4

AN OCCURRENCE AT OWL CREEK BRIDGE

BY AMBROSE BIERCE

Convicted as a spy, a Confederate prisoner faces hanging. And then . . .

A man stood upon a railroad bridge in northern Alabama, looking down into the swift water twenty feet below. The man's hands were behind his back, the wrists bound with a cord. A rope closely encircled his neck. It was attached to a stout cross-timber above his head and the slack fell to the level of his knees. Some loose boards laid upon the sleepers supporting the metals of the railway supplied a footing for him and his executioners—two private soldiers of the Federal army, directed by a sergeant who in civil life may have been a deputy sheriff. At a short remove upon the same temporary platform was an officer in the uniform of his rank, armed. He was a captain. A sentinel at each end of the bridge stood with his rifle in the position known as "support," that is to say, vertical in front of the left shoulder, the hammer resting on the forearm thrown straight across the chest—a formal and unnatural position, enforcing an erect carriage of the body. It did not appear to be the duty of these two men to know what was occurring at the center of the bridge; they merely blockaded the two ends of the foot planking that traversed it.

Beyond one of the sentinels nobody was in sight; the railroad ran straight away into a forest for a hundred yards, then, curving, was lost to view. Doubtless there was an outpost farther along. The other bank of the stream was open ground—a gentle activity topped with a stockade of vertical tree trunks, loopholed for rifles, with a single embrasure through which protruded the muzzle of a brass cannon commanding the bridge. Midway of the slope between bridge and fort were the spectators—a single company of infantry in line, at "parade rest," the butts of the rifles on the ground, the barrels inclining slightly backward against the right shoulder, the hands crossed upon the stock. A lieutenant stood at the right of the line, the point of his sword upon the ground, his left hand resting upon his right. Excepting the group of four at the center of the bridge, not a man moved. The company faced the bridge, staring stonily, motionless. The sentinels, facing the banks of the stream, might have been statues to adorn the bridge. The captain stood with folded arms, silent, observing the work of his subordinates, but making no sign. Death is a dignitary who when he comes announced is to be received with formal manifestations of respect, even by those most familiar with him. In the code of military etiquette silence and fixity are forms of deference.

The man who was engaged in being hanged was apparently about thirty-five years of age. He was a civilian, if one might judge from his habit, which was that of a planter. His features were good—a straight nose, firm mouth, broad forehead, from which his long, dark hair was combed straight back, falling behind his ears to the collar of his well-fitting frock-coat. He wore a mustache and pointed beard, but no whiskers; his eyes were large and dark gray, and had a kindly expression which one would hardly have expected in one whose neck was in the hemp. Evidently this was no vulgar assassin. The liberal military code makes provision for hanging many kinds of persons, and gentlemen are not excluded.

The preparations being complete, the two private soldiers stepped aside and each drew away the plank upon which he had been standing. The sergeant turned to the captain, saluted and placed himself immediately behind that officer, who in turn moved apart one pace. These movements left the condemned man and the sergeant standing on the two ends of the same plank, which spanned three of the cross-ties of the bridge. The end upon which the civilian stood almost, but not quite, reached a fourth. This plank had been held in place by the weight of the captain; it was now held by that of the sergeant. At a signal from the former the latter would step aside, the plank would tilt, and the condemned man go down between two ties. The arrangement commended itself to his judgment as simple and effective. His face had not been covered nor his eyes bandaged. He looked a moment at his "unsteadfast footing," then let his gaze wander to the swirling water of the stream racing madly beneath his feet. A piece of dancing driftwood caught his attention and his eyes followed it down the current. How slowly it appeared to move!

What a sluggish stream!

He closed his eyes in order to fix his last thoughts upon his wife and children. The water, touched to gold by the early sun, the brooding mists under the banks at some distance down the stream, the fort, the soldiers, the piece of driftwood—all had distracted him. And now he became conscious of a new disturbance. Striking through the thought of his dear ones was a sound which he could neither ignore nor understand, a sharp, distinct, metallic percussion like the stroke of a blacksmith's hammer upon the anvil; it had the same ringing quality. He wondered what it was, and whether immeasurably distant or nearby—it seemed both. Its recurrence was regular, but as slow as the tolling of a death knell. He awaited each stroke with impatience and—he knew not why—apprehension. The intervals of silence grew progressively longer; the delays became maddening. With their greater infrequency the sounds increased in strength and sharpness. They hurt his ear like the thrust of a knife; he feared he would shriek. What he heard was the ticking of his watch. He unclosed his eyes and saw again the water below him.

"If I could free my hands," he thought, "I might throw off the noose and spring into the stream. By diving I could evade the bullets and, swimming vigorously, reach the bank, take to the woods and get away home. My home, thank God, is as yet outside their lines; my wife and little ones are still beyond the invader's farthest advance."

As these thoughts, which have here to be set down in words, were flashed into the doomed man's brain rather than evolved from it, the captain nodded to the sergeant. The sergeant stepped aside.

Peyton Farquhar was a well-to-do planter, of an old and highly respected Alabama family. Being a slave owner and like other slave owners a politician he was naturally an original secessionist and ardently devoted to the Southern cause. Circumstances of an imperious nature, which it is unnecessary to relate here, had prevented him from taking service with the gallant army that had fought the disastrous campaigns ending with the fall of Corinth, and he chafed under the inglorious restraint, longing for the release of his energies, the larger life of the soldier, the opportunity for distinction. That opportunity, he felt, would come, as it comes to all in war time. Meanwhile he did what he could. No service was too humble for him to perform in aid of the South, no adventure too perilous for him to undertake if consistent with the character of a civilian who was at heart a soldier, and who in good faith and without too much qualification assented to at least a part of the frankly villainous dictum that all is fair in love and war.

One evening while Farquhar and his wife were sitting on a rustic bench near the entrance to his grounds, a gray-clad soldier rode up to the gate and asked for a drink of water. Mrs. Farquhar was only too happy to serve him with her own white hands. While she was fetching the water her husband approached the dusty horseman and inquired eagerly for news from the front.

"The Yanks are repairing the railroads," said the man, "and are getting ready for another advance. They have reached the Owl Creek bridge, put it in order, and built a stockade on the north bank. The commandant has issued an order, which is posted everywhere, declaring that any civilian caught interfering with the railroad, its bridges, tunnels, or trains, will be summarily hanged. I saw the order."

"How far is it to the Owl Creek bridge?" Farquhar asked.

"About thirty miles."

"Is there no force on this side the creek?"

"Only a picket post half a mile out, on the railroad, and a single sentinel at this end of the bridge."

"Suppose a man—a civilian and student of hanging—should elude the picket post and perhaps get the better of the sentinel," said Farquhar, smiling, "what could he accomplish?"

The soldier reflected. "I was there a month ago," he replied. "I observed that the flood of last winter had lodged a great quantity of driftwood against the wooden pier at this end of the bridge. It is now dry and would burn like tow [rapidly]."

The lady had now brought the water, which the soldier drank. He thanked her ceremoniously, bowed to her husband, and rode away. An hour later, after nightfall, he repassed the plantation, going northward in the direction from which he had come. He was a Federal scout.

As Peyton Farquhar fell straight downward through the bridge he lost consciousness and was as one already dead. From this state he was awakened—ages later, it seemed to him—by the pain of a sharp pressure upon his throat, followed by a sense of suffocation. Keen, poignant agonies seemed to shoot from his neck downward through every fibre of his body and limbs. These pains appeared to flash along well-defined lines of ramification and to beat with an inconceivably rapid periodicity. They seemed like streams of pulsating fire heating him to an intolerable temperature. As to his head, he was conscious of nothing but a feeling of fulness—of congestion. These sensations were unaccompanied by thought. The intellectual part of his nature was already effaced; he had power only to feel, and feeling was torment.

He was conscious of motion. Encompassed in a luminous cloud, of which he was now merely the fiery heart, without material substance, he swung through unthinkable arcs of oscillation, like a vast pendulum. Then all at once, with terrible suddenness, the light about him shot upward with the noise of a loud plash; a frightful roaring was in his ears, and all was cold and dark. The power of thought was restored; he knew that the rope had broken and he had fallen into the stream. There was no additional strangulation; the noose about his neck was already suffocating him and kept the water from his lungs. To die of hanging at the bottom of a river!—the idea seemed to him ludicrous.

He opened his eyes in the darkness and saw above him a gleam of light, but how distant, how inaccessible! He was still sinking, for the light became fainter and fainter until it was a mere glimmer. Then it began to grow and brighten, and he knew that he was rising toward the surface—knew it with reluctance, for he was now very comfortable. "To be hanged and drowned," he thought, "that is not so bad; but I do not wish to be shot. No; I will not be shot; that is not fair."

He was not conscious of an effort, but a sharp pain in his wrist apprised him that he was trying to free his hands. He gave the struggle his attention, as an idler might observe the feat of a juggler, without interest in the outcome. What splendid effort!—what magnificent, what superhuman strength! Ah, that was a fine endeavor! Bravo! The cord fell away; his arms parted and floated upward, the hands dimly seen on each side in the growing light. He watched them with a new interest as first one and then the other pounced upon the noose at his neck. They tore it away and thrust it fiercely aside, its undulations resembling those of a water-snake. "Put it back, put it back!" He thought he shouted these words to his hands, for the undoing of the noose had been succeeded by the direst pang that he had yet experienced. His neck ached horribly; his brain was on fire; his heart, which had been fluttering faintly, gave a great leap, trying to force itself out at his mouth. His whole body was racked and wrenched with an insupportable anguish! But his disobedient hands gave no heed to the command. They beat the water vigorously with quick, downward strokes, forcing him to the surface. He felt his head emerge; his eyes were blinded by the sunlight; his chest expanded convulsively, and with a supreme and crowning agony his lungs engulfed a great draught of air, which instantly he expelled in a shriek!

He was now in full possession of his physical senses. They were, indeed, preternaturally keen and alert. Something in the awful disturbance of his organic system had so exalted and refined them that they made record of things never before perceived. He felt the ripples upon his face and heard their separate sounds as they struck. He looked at the forest on the bank of the stream, saw the individual trees, the leaves and the veining of each leaf—saw the very insects upon them: the locusts, the brilliant-bodied flies, the gray spiders stretching their webs from twig to twig. He noted the prismatic colors in all the dewdrops upon a million blades of grass. The humming of the gnats that danced above the eddies of the stream, the beating of the dragon-flies' wings, the strokes of the water-spiders' legs, like oars which had lifted their boat—all these made audible music. A fish slid along beneath his eyes and he heard the rush of its body parting the water.

He had come to the surface facing down the stream; in a moment the visible world seemed to wheel slowly round, himself the pivotal point, and he saw the bridge, the fort, the soldiers upon the bridge, the captain, the sergeant, the two privates, his executioners. They were in silhouette against the blue sky. They shouted and gesticulated, pointing at him. The captain had drawn his pistol, but did not fire; the others were unarmed. Their movements were grotesque and horrible, their forms gigantic.

Suddenly he heard a sharp report and something struck the water smartly within a few inches of his head, spattering his face with spray. He heard a second report, and saw one of the sentinels with his rifle at his shoulder, a light cloud of blue smoke rising from the muzzle. The man in the water saw the eye of the man on the bridge gazing into his own through the sights of the rifle. He observed that it was a gray eye and remembered having read that gray eyes were keenest, and that all famous marksmen had them. Nevertheless, this one had missed.

A counter-swirl had caught Farquhar and turned him half round; he was again looking into the forest on the bank opposite the fort. The sound of a clear, high voice in a monotonous singsong now rang out behind him and came across the water with a distinctness that pierced and subdued all other sounds, even the beating of the ripples in his ears. Although no soldier, he had frequented camps enough to know the dread significance of that deliberate, drawling, aspirated chant; the lieutenant on shore was taking a part in the morning's work. How coldly and pitilessly—with what an even, calm intonation, presaging, and enforcing tranquility in the men—with what accurately measured intervals fell those cruel words:

"Attention, company! . . . Shoulder arms! . . . Ready! . . . Aim! . . . Fire!"

Farquhar dived—dived as deeply as he could. The water roared in his ears like the voice of Niagara, yet he heard the dulled thunder of the volley and, rising again toward the surface, met shining bits of metal, singularly flattened, oscillating slowly downward. Some of them touched him on the face and hands, then fell away, continuing their descent. One lodged between his collar and neck; it was uncomfortably warm and he snatched it out.

As he rose to the surface, gasping for breath, he saw that he had been a long time under water; he was perceptibly farther downstream—nearer to safety. The soldiers had almost finished reloading; the metal ramrods flashed all at once in the sunshine as they were drawn from the barrels, turned in the air, and thrust into their sockets. The two sentinels fired again, independently and ineffectually.

The hunted man saw all this over his shoulder; he was now swimming vigorously with the current. His brain was as energetic as his arms and legs; he thought with the rapidity of lightning.

"The officer," he reasoned, "will not make that martinet's error a second time. It is as easy to dodge a volley as a single shot. He has probably already given the command to fire at will. God help me, I cannot dodge them all!"

An appalling plash within two yards of him was followed by a loud, rushing sound, *diminuendo*, which seemed to travel back through the air to the fort and died in an explosion which stirred the very river to its deeps! A rising sheet of water curved over him, fell down upon him, blinded him, strangled him! The cannon had taken a hand in the game. As he shook his head free from the commotion of the smitten water he heard the deflected shot humming through the air ahead, and in an instant it was cracking and smashing the branches in the forest beyond.

"They will not do that again," he thought; "the next time they will use a charge of grape. I must keep my eye upon the gun; the smoke will apprise me—the report arrives too late; it lags behind the missile. That is a good gun."

Suddenly he felt himself whirled round and round—spinning like a top. The water, the banks, the forests, the now distant bridge, fort and men—all were commingled and blurred. Objects were represented by their colors only; circular horizontal streaks of color—that was all he saw. He had been caught in a vortex and was being whirled on with a velocity of advance and gyration that made him giddy and sick. In a few moments he was flung upon the gravel at the foot of the left bank of the stream—the southern bank—and behind a projecting point which concealed him from his enemies. The sudden arrest of his motion, the abrasion of one of his hands on the gravel, restored him, and he wept with delight. He dug his fingers into the sand, threw it over himself in handfuls, and audibly blessed it. It looked like diamonds, rubies, emeralds; he could think of nothing beautiful which it did not resemble. The trees upon the bank were giant garden plants; he noted a definite order in their arrangement, inhaled the fragrance of their blooms. A strange, roseate light shone through the spaces among their trunks and the wind made in their branches the music of Aeolian harps. He had no wish to perfect his escape—was content to remain in that enchanting spot until retaken.

A whiz and rattle of grapeshot among the branches high above his head roused him from his dream. The baffled cannoneer had fired him a random farewell. He sprang to his feet, rushed up the sloping bank, and plunged into the forest.

All that day he traveled, laying his course by the rounding sun. The forest seemed interminable; nowhere did he discover a break in it, not even a woodman's road. He had not known that he lived in so wild a region. There was something uncanny in the revelation.

By night fall he was fatigued, footsore, famishing. The thought of his wife and children urged him on. At last he found a road which led him in what he knew to be the right direction. It was as wide and straight as a city street, yet it seemed untraveled. No fields bordered it, no dwelling anywhere. Not so much as the barking of a dog suggested human habitation. The black bodies of the trees formed a straight wall on both sides, terminating on the horizon in a point, like a diagram in a lesson in perspective. Overhead, as he looked up through this rift in the wood, shone great golden stars looking unfamiliar and grouped in strange constellations. He was sure they were arranged in some order which had a secret and malign significance. The wood on either side was full of singular noises, among which—once, twice, and again, he distinctly heard whispers in an unknown tongue.

His neck was in pain and lifting his hand to it he found it horribly swollen. He knew that it had a circle of black where the rope had bruised it. His eyes felt congested; he could no longer close them. His tongue was swollen with thirst; he relieved its fever by thrusting it forward from between his teeth into the cold air. How softly the turf had carpeted the untraveled avenue—he could no longer feel the roadway beneath his feet!

Doubtless, despite his suffering, he had fallen asleep while walking, for now he sees another scene—perhaps he has merely recovered from a delirium. He stands at the gate of his own home. All is as he left it, and all bright and beautiful in the morning sunshine. He must have traveled the entire night. As he pushes open the gate and passes up the wide white walk, he sees a flutter of female garments; his wife, looking fresh and cool and sweet, steps down from the veranda to meet him. At the bottom of the steps she stands waiting, with a smile of ineffable joy, an attitude of matchless grace and dignity. Ah, how beautiful she is! He springs forward with extended arms. As he is about to clasp her he feels a stunning blow upon the back of the neck; a blinding white light blazes all about him with a sound like the shock of a cannon—then all is darkness and silence!

Peyton Farquhar was dead; his body, with a broken neck, swung gently from side to side beneath the timbers of the Owl Creek bridge.

5

THE PIT AND THE PENDULUM

BY EDGAR ALLAN POE

"The Pit and the Pendulum" was first published in 1842 in a literary annual. As one of the most widely praised short stories of Edgar Allan Poe (1809–1849), it showcases Poe's immense talent, particularly in tales of mystery and dark suspense.

I was sick—sick unto death with that long agony; and when they at length unbound me, and I was permitted to sit, I felt that my senses were leaving me. The sentence—the dread sentence of death—was the last of distinct accentuation which reached my ears. After that, the sound of the inquisitorial voices seemed merged in one dreamy indeterminate hum. It conveyed to my soul the idea of *revolution*—perhaps from its association in fancy with the burr of a mill wheel. This only for a brief period, for presently I heard no more. Yet, for a while, I saw—but with how terrible an exaggeration! I saw the lips of the black-robed judges. They appeared to me white—whiter than the sheet upon which I trace these words—and thin even to grotesqueness; thin with the intensity of their expression of firmness—of immoveable resolution—of stern contempt of human torture. I saw that the decrees of what to me was Fate, were still issuing from those lips. I saw them writhe with a deadly locution. I saw them fashion the syllables of my name; and I shuddered because no sound succeeded. I saw, too, for a few moments of delirious horror, the soft and nearly imperceptible waving of the sable draperies which enwrapped the walls of the apartment. And then my vision fell upon the seven tall candles upon the table. At first they wore the aspect of charity, and seemed white and slender angels who would save me; but then, all at once, there came a most deadly nausea over my spirit, and I felt every fibre in my frame thrill as if I had touched the wire of a galvanic battery, while the angel forms became meaningless spectres, with heads of flame, and I saw that from them there would be no help. And then there stole into my fancy, like a rich musical note, the thought of what sweet rest there must be in the grave. The thought came gently and stealthily, and it seemed long before it attained full appreciation; but just as my spirit came at length properly to feel and entertain it, the figures of the judges vanished, as if magically, from before me; the tall candles sank into nothingness; their flames went out utterly; the blackness of darkness supervened; all sensations appeared swallowed up in a mad rushing descent as of the soul into Hades. Then silence, and stillness, night were the universe.

I had swooned; but still will not say that all of consciousness was lost. What of it there remained I will not attempt to define, or even to describe; yet all was not lost. In the deepest slumber—no! In delirium—no! In a swoon—no! In death—no! even in the grave all is not lost. Else there is no immortality for man. Arousing from the most profound of slumbers, we break the gossamer web of some dream. Yet in a second afterward, (so frail may that web have been) we remember not that we have dreamed. In the return to life from the swoon there are two stages; first, that of the sense of mental or spiritual; secondly, that of the sense of physical, existence. It seems probable that if, upon reaching the second stage, we could recall the impressions of the first, we should find these impressions eloquent in memories of the gulf beyond. And that gulf is—what? How at least shall we distinguish its shadows from those of the tomb? But if the impressions of what I have termed the first stage are not, at will, recalled, yet, after long interval, do they not come unbidden, while we marvel whence they come? He who has never swooned, is not he who finds strange palaces and wildly familiar faces in coals that glow; is not he who beholds floating in mid-air the sad visions that the many may not view; is not he who ponders over the perfume of some novel flower; is not he whose brain grows bewildered with the meaning of some musical cadence which has never before arrested his attention.

Amid frequent and thoughtful endeavors to remember; amid earnest struggles to regather some token of the state of seeming nothingness into which my soul had lapsed, there have been moments when I have dreamed of success; there have been brief, very brief periods when I have conjured up remembrances which the lucid reason of a later epoch assures me could have had reference only to that condition of seeming unconsciousness. These shadows of memory tell, indistinctly, of tall figures that lifted and bore me in silence down—down—still down—till a hideous dizziness oppressed me at the mere idea of the interminableness of the descent. They tell also of a vague horror at my heart, on account of that heart's unnatural stillness. Then comes a sense of sudden motionlessness throughout all things; as if those who bore me (a ghastly train!) had outrun, in their descent, the limits of the limitless, and paused from the wearisomeness of their toil. After this I call to mind flatness and dampness; and then all is madness—the madness of a memory which busies itself among forbidden things.

Very suddenly there came back to my soul motion and sound—the tumultuous motion of the heart, and, in my ears, the sound of its beating. Then a pause in which all is blank. Then again sound, and motion, and touch—a tingling sensation pervading my frame. Then the mere consciousness of existence, without thought—a condition which lasted long. Then, very suddenly, thought, and shuddering terror, and earnest endeavor to comprehend my true state. Then a strong desire to lapse into insensibility. Then a rushing revival of soul and a successful effort to move. And now a full memory of the trial, of the judges, of the sable draperies, of the sentence, of the sickness, of the swoon. Then entire forgetfulness of all that followed; of all that a later day and much earnestness of endeavor have enabled me vaguely to recall.

So far, I had not opened my eyes. I felt that I lay upon my back, unbound. I reached out my hand, and it fell heavily upon something damp and hard. There I suffered it to remain for many minutes, while I strove to imagine where and what I could be. I longed, yet dared not to employ my vision. I dreaded the first glance at objects around me. It was not that I feared to look upon things horrible, but that I grew aghast lest there should be nothing to see. At length, with a wild desperation at heart, I quickly unclosed my eyes. My worst thoughts, then, were confirmed. The blackness of eternal night encompassed me. I struggled for breath. The intensity of the darkness seemed to oppress and stifle me. The atmosphere was intolerably close. I still lay quietly, and made effort to exercise my reason. I brought to mind the inquisitorial proceedings, and attempted from that point to deduce my real condition. The sentence had passed; and it appeared to me that a very long interval of time had since elapsed. Yet not for a moment did I suppose myself actually dead. Such a supposition, notwithstanding what we read in fiction, is altogether inconsistent with real existence;—but where and in what state was I? The condemned to death, I knew, perished usually at the autos-da-fé, and one of these had been held on the very night of the day of my trial. Had I been remanded to my dungeon, to await the next sacrifice, which would not take place for many months? This I at once saw could not be. Victims had been in immediate demand. Moreover, my dungeon, as well as all the condemned cells at Toledo, had stone floors, and light was not altogether excluded.

A fearful idea now suddenly drove the blood in torrents upon my heart, and for a brief period, I once more relapsed into insensibility. Upon recovering, I at once started to my feet, trembling convulsively in every fibre. I thrust my arms wildly above and around me in all directions. I felt nothing; yet dreaded to move a step, lest I should be impeded by the walls of a tomb. Perspiration burst from every pore, and stood in cold big beads upon my forehead. The agony of suspense grew at length intolerable, and I cautiously moved forward, with my arms extended, and my eyes straining from their sockets, in the hope of catching some faint ray of light. I proceeded for many paces; but still all was blackness and vacancy. I breathed more freely. It seemed evident that mine was not, at least, the most hideous of fates.

And now, as I still continued to step cautiously onward, there came thronging upon my recollection a thousand vague rumors of the horrors of Toledo. Of the dungeons there had been strange things narrated—fables I had always deemed them—but yet strange, and too ghastly to repeat, save in a whisper. Was I left to perish of starvation in this subterranean world of darkness; or what fate, perhaps even more fearful, awaited me? That the result would be death, and a death of more than customary bitterness, I knew too well the character of my judges to doubt. The mode and the hour were all that occupied or distracted me.

My outstretched hands at length encountered some solid obstruction. It was a wall, seemingly of stone masonry—very smooth, slimy, and cold. I followed it up; stepping with all the careful distrust with which certain antique narratives had inspired me. This process, however, afforded me no means of ascertaining the dimensions of my dungeon; as I might make its circuit, and return to the point whence I set out, without being aware of the fact; so perfectly uniform seemed the wall. I therefore sought the knife which had been in my pocket, when led into the inquisitorial chamber; but it was gone; my clothes had been exchanged for a wrapper of coarse serge. I had thought of forcing the blade in some minute crevice of the masonry, so as to identify my point of departure. The difficulty, nevertheless, was but trivial; although, in the disorder of my fancy, it seemed at first insuperable. I tore a part of the hem from the robe and placed the fragment at full length, and at right angles to the wall. In groping my way around the prison, I could not fail to encounter this rag upon completing the circuit. So, at least I thought: but I had not counted upon the extent of the dungeon, or upon my own weakness. The ground was moist and slippery. I staggered onward for some time, when I stumbled and fell. My excessive fatigue induced me to remain prostrate; and sleep soon overtook me as I lay.

Upon awaking, and stretching forth an arm, I found beside me a loaf and a pitcher with water. I was too much exhausted to reflect upon this circumstance, but ate and drank with avidity. Shortly afterward, I resumed my tour around the prison, and with much toil came at last upon the fragment of the serge. Up to the period when I fell I had counted fifty-two paces, and upon resuming my walk, I had counted forty-eight more—when I arrived at the rag. There were in all, then, a hundred paces; and, admitting two paces to the yard, I presumed the dungeon to be fifty yards in circuit. I had met, however, with many angles in the wall, and thus I could form no guess at the shape of the vault, for vault I could not help supposing it to be.

I had little object—certainly no hope—in these researches; but a vague curiosity prompted me to continue them. Quitting the wall, I resolved to cross the area of the enclosure. At first I proceeded with extreme caution, for the floor, although seemingly of solid material, was treacherous with slime. At length, however, I took courage, and did not hesitate to step firmly; endeavoring to cross in as direct a line as possible. I had advanced some ten or twelve paces in this manner, when the remnant of the torn hem of my robe became entangled between my legs. I stepped on it, and fell violently on my face.

In the confusion attending my fall, I did not immediately apprehend a somewhat startling circumstance, which yet, in a few seconds afterward, and while I still lay prostrate, arrested my attention. It was this: my chin rested upon the floor of the prison, but my lips and the upper portion of my head, although seemingly at a less elevation than the chin, touched nothing. At the same time my forehead seemed bathed in a clammy vapor, and the peculiar smell of decayed fungus arose to my nostrils. I put forward my arm, and shuddered to find that I had fallen at the very brink of a circular pit, whose extent, of course, I had no means of ascertaining at the moment. Groping about the masonry just below the margin, I succeeded in dislodging a small fragment, and let it fall into the abyss. For many seconds I hearkened to its reverberations as it dashed against the sides of the chasm in its descent; at length there was a sullen plunge into water, succeeded by loud echoes. At the same moment there came a sound resembling the quick opening, and as rapid closing of a door overhead, while a faint gleam of light flashed suddenly through the gloom, and as suddenly faded away.

I saw clearly the doom which had been prepared for me, and congratulated myself upon the timely accident by which I had escaped. Another step before my fall, and the world had seen me no more. And the death just avoided, was of that very character which I had regarded as fabulous and frivolous in the tales respecting the Inquisition. To the victims of its tyranny, there was the choice of death with its direst physical agonies, or death with its most hideous moral horrors. I had been reserved for the latter. By long suffering my nerves had been unstrung, until I trembled at the sound of my own voice, and had become in every respect a fitting subject for the species of torture which awaited me.

Shaking in every limb, I groped my way back to the wall—resolving there to perish rather than risk the terrors of the wells, of which my imagination now pictured many in various positions about the dungeon. In other conditions of mind I might have had courage to end my misery at once by a plunge into one of these abysses; but now I was the veriest of cowards. Neither could I forget what I had read of these pits—that the sudden extinction of life formed no part of their most horrible plan.

Agitation of spirit kept me awake for many long hours, but at length I again slumbered. Upon arousing, I found by my side, as before, a loaf and a pitcher of water. A burning thirst consumed me, and I emptied the vessel at a draught. It must have been drugged—for scarcely had I drunk, before I became irresistibly drowsy. A deep sleep fell upon me—a sleep like that of death. How long it lasted of course, I know not; but when, once again, I unclosed my eyes, the objects around me were visible. By a wild sulphurous lustre, the origin of which I could not at first determine, I was enabled to see the extent and aspect of the prison.

In its size I had been greatly mistaken. The whole circuit of its walls did not exceed twenty-five yards. For some minutes this fact occasioned me a world of vain trouble; vain indeed! for what could be of less importance, under the terrible circumstances which environed me, then the mere dimensions of my dungeon? But my soul took a wild interest in trifles, and I busied myself in endeavors to account for the error I had committed in my measurement. The truth at length flashed upon me. In my first attempt at exploration I had counted fifty-two paces, up to the period when I fell; I must then have been within a pace or two of the fragment of serge; in fact, I had nearly performed the circuit of the vault. I then slept—and, upon awaking, I must have returned upon my steps—thus supposing the circuit nearly double what it actually was. My confusion of mind prevented me from observing that I began my tour with the wall to the left, and ended it with the wall to the right.

I had been deceived, too, in respect to the shape of the enclosure. In feeling my way I had found many angles, and thus deduced an idea of great irregularity; so potent is the effect of total darkness upon one arousing from lethargy or sleep! The angles were simply those of a few slight depressions, or niches, at odd intervals. The general shape of the prison was square. What I had taken for masonry seemed now to be iron, or some other metal, in huge plates, whose sutures or joints occasioned the depression. The entire surface of this metallic enclosure was rudely daubed in all the hideous and repulsive devices to which the charnel superstition of the monks has given rise. The figures of fiends in aspects of menace, with skeleton forms, and other more really fearful images, overspread and disfigured the walls. I observed that the outlines of these monstrosities were sufficiently distinct, but that the colors seemed faded and blurred, as if from the effects of a damp atmosphere. I now noticed the floor, too, which was of stone. In the centre yawned the circular pit from whose jaws I had escaped; but it was the only one in the dungeon.

All this I saw indistinctly and by much effort—for my personal condition had been greatly changed during slumber. I now lay upon my back, and at full length, on a species of low framework of wood. To this I was securely bound by a long strap resembling a surcingle. It passed in many convolutions about my limbs and body, leaving at liberty only my head, and my left arm to such extent that I could, by dint of much exertion, supply myself with food from an earthen dish which lay by my side on the floor. I saw, to my horror, that the pitcher had been removed. I say to my horror—for I was consumed with intolerable thirst. This thirst it appeared to be the design of my persecutors to stimulate—for the food in the dish was meat pungently seasoned.

Looking upward, I surveyed the ceiling of my prison. It was some thirty or forty feet overhead, and constructed much as the side walls. In one of its panels a very singular figure riveted my whole attention. It was the painted figure of Time as he is commonly represented, save that, in lieu of a scythe, he held what, at a casual glance, I supposed to be the pictured image of a huge pendulum such as we see on antique clocks. There was something, however, in the appearance of this machine which caused me to regard it more attentively. While I gazed directly upward at it (for its position was immediately over my own) I fancied that I saw it in motion. In an instant afterward the fancy was confirmed. Its sweep was brief, and of course slow. I watched it for some minutes, somewhat in fear, but more in wonder. Wearied at length with observing its dull movement, I turned my eyes upon the other objects in the cell.

A slight noise attracted my notice, and, looking to the floor, I saw several enormous rats traversing it. They had issued from the well, which lay just within view to my right. Even then, while I gazed, they came up in troops, hurriedly, with ravenous eyes, allured by the scent of the meat. From this it required much effort and attention to scare them away.

It might have been half an hour, perhaps even an hour, (for I could take but imperfect note of time) before I again cast my eyes upward. What I then saw confounded and amazed me. The sweep of the pendulum had increased in extent by nearly a yard. As a natural consequence, its velocity was also much greater. But what mainly disturbed me was the idea that had perceptibly descended. I now observed—with what horror it is needless to say—that its nether extremity was formed of a crescent of glittering steel, about a foot in length from horn to horn; the horns upward, and the under edge evidently as keen as that of a razor. Like a razor also, it seemed massy and heavy, tapering from the edge into a solid and broad structure above. It was appended to a weighty rod of brass, and the whole hissed as it swung through the air.

I could no longer doubt the doom prepared for me by monkish ingenuity in torture. My cognizance of the pit had become known to the inquisitorial agents—*the pit*, whose horrors had been destined for so bold a recusant as myself—the pit, typical of hell, and regarded by rumor as the Ultima Thule of all their punishments. The plunge into this pit I had avoided by the merest of accidents; I knew that surprise, or entrapment into torment, formed an important portion of all the grotesquerie of these dungeon deaths. Having failed to fall, it was no part of the demon plan to hurl me into the abyss; and thus (there being no alternative) a different and a milder destruction awaited me. Milder! I half smiled in my agony as I thought of such application of such a term.

What boots it to tell of the long, long hours of horror more than mortal, during which I counted the rushing vibrations of the steel! Inch by inch—line by line—with a descent only appreciable at intervals that seemed ages—down and still down it came! Days passed—it might have been that many days passed—ere it swept so closely over me as to fan me with its acrid breath. The odor of the sharp steel forced itself into my nostrils. I prayed—I wearied heaven with my prayer for its more speedy descent. I grew frantically mad, and struggled to force myself upward against the sweep of the fearful scimitar. And then I fell suddenly calm, and lay smiling at the glittering death, as a child at some rare bauble.

There was another interval of utter insensibility; it was brief; for, upon again lapsing into life there had been no perceptible descent in the pendulum. But it might have been long; for I knew there were demons who took note of my swoon, and who could have arrested the vibration at pleasure. Upon my recovery, too, I felt very—oh! inexpressibly—sick and weak, as if through long inanition. Even amid the agonies of that period, the human nature craved food. With painful effort I outstretched my left arm as far as my bonds permitted, and took possession of the small remnant which had been spared me by the rats. As I put a portion of it within my lips, there rushed to my mind a half formed thought of joy—of hope. Yet what business had I with hope? It was, as I say, a half formed thought—man has many such, which are never completed. I felt that it was of joy—of hope; but felt also that it had perished in its formation. In vain I struggled to perfect—to regain it. Long suffering had nearly annihilated all my ordinary powers of mind. I was an imbecile—an idiot.

The vibration of the pendulum was at right angles to my length. I saw that the crescent was designed to cross the region of the heart. It would fray the serge of my robe—it would return and repeat its operations—again—and again. Notwithstanding its terrifically wide sweep (some thirty feet or more) and the hissing vigor of its descent, sufficient to sunder these very walls of iron, still the fraying of my robe would be all that, for several minutes, it would accomplish. And at this thought I paused. I dared not go farther than this reflection. I dwelt upon it with a pertinacity of attention—as if, in so dwelling, I could arrest here the descent of the steel. I forced myself to ponder upon the sound of the crescent as it should pass across the garment—upon the peculiar thrilling sensation which the friction of cloth produces on the nerves. I pondered upon all this frivolity until my teeth were on edge.

Down—steadily down it crept. I took a frenzied pleasure in contrasting its downward with its lateral velocity. To the right—to the left—far and wide—with the shriek of a damned spirit! to my heart with the stealthy pace of the tiger! I alternately laughed and howled as the one or the other idea grew predominant.

Down—certainly, relentlessly down! It vibrated within three inches of my bosom! I struggled violently, furiously, to free my left arm. This was free only from the elbow to the hand. I could reach the latter, from the platter beside me, to my mouth, with great effort, but no farther. Could I have broken the fastenings above the elbow, I would have seized and attempted to arrest the pendulum. I might as well have attempted to arrest an avalanche!

Down—still unceasingly—still inevitably down! I gasped and struggled at each vibration. I shrunk convulsively at its every sweep. My eyes followed its outward or upward whirls with the eagerness of the most unmeaning despair; they closed themselves spasmodically at the descent, although death would have been a relief, oh, how unspeakable! Still I quivered in every nerve to think how slight a sinking of the machinery would precipitate that keen, glistening axe upon my bosom. It was hope that prompted the nerve to quiver—the frame to shrink. It was hope—the hope that triumphs on the rack—that whispers to the death-condemned even in the dungeons of the Inquisition.

I saw that some ten or twelve vibrations would bring the steel in actual contact with my robe, and with this observation there suddenly came over my spirit all the keen, collected calmness of despair. For the first time during many hours—or perhaps days—I thought. It now occurred to me that the bandage, or surcingle, which enveloped me, was unique. I was tied by no separate cord. The first stroke of the razorlike crescent athwart any portion of the band, would so detach it that it might be unwound from my person by means of my left hand. But how fearful, in that case, the proximity of the steel! The result of the slightest struggle how deadly! Was it likely, moreover, that the minions of the torturer had not foreseen and provided for this possibility? Was it probable that the bandage crossed my bosom in the track of the pendulum? Dreading to find my faint, and, as it seemed, my last hope frustrated, I so far elevated my head as to obtain a distinct view of my breast. The surcingle enveloped my limbs and body close in all directions—save in the path of the destroying crescent.

Scarcely had I dropped my head back into its original position, when there flashed upon my mind what I cannot better describe than as the unformed half of that idea of deliverance to which I have previously alluded, and of which a moiety only floated indeterminately through my brain when I raised food to my burning lips. The whole thought was now present—feeble, scarcely sane, scarcely definite—but still entire. I proceeded at once, with the nervous energy of despair, to attempt its execution.

For many hours the immediate vicinity of the low framework upon which I lay had been literally swarming with rats. They were wild, bold, ravenous—their red eyes glaring upon me as if they waited but for motionlessness on my part to make me their prey. "To what food," I thought, "have they been accustomed in the well?"

They had devoured, in spite of all my efforts to prevent them, all but a small remnant of the contents of the dish. I had fallen into an habitual see-saw, or wave of the hand about the platter; and, at length, the unconscious uniformity of the movement deprived it of effect. In their voracity the vermin frequently fastened their sharp fangs in my fingers. With the particles of the oily and spicy viand which now remained, I thoroughly rubbed the bandage wherever I could reach it; then, raising my hand from the floor, I lay breathlessly still.

At first the ravenous animals were startled and terrified at the change—at the cessation of movement. They shrank alarmedly back; many sought the well. But this was only for a moment. I had not counted in vain upon their voracity. Observing that I remained without motion, one or two of the boldest leaped upon the frame-work, and smelt at the surcingle. This seemed the signal for a general rush. Forth from the well they hurried in fresh troops. They clung to the wood—they overran it, and leaped in hundreds upon my person. The measured movement of the pendulum disturbed them not at all. Avoiding its strokes they busied themselves with the anointed bandage. They pressed—they swarmed upon me in ever accumulating heaps. They writhed upon my throat; their cold lips sought my own; I was half stifled by their thronging pressure; disgust, for which the world has no name, swelled my bosom, and chilled, with a heavy clamminess, my heart. Yet one minute, and I felt that the struggle would be over. Plainly I perceived the loosening of the bandage. I knew that in more than one place it must be already severed. With a more than human resolution I lay still.

Nor had I erred in my calculations—nor had I endured in vain. I at length felt that I was free. The surcingle hung in ribands from my body. But the stroke of the pendulum already pressed upon my bosom. It had divided the serge of the robe. It had cut through the linen beneath. Twice again it swung, and a sharp sense of pain shot through every nerve. But the moment of escape had arrived. At a wave of my hand my deliverers hurried tumultuously away. With a steady movement—cautious, sidelong, shrinking, and slow—I slid from the embrace of the bandage and beyond the reach of the scimitar. For the moment, at least, I was free.

Free!—and in the grasp of the Inquisition! I had scarcely stepped from my wooden bed of horror upon the stone floor of the prison, when the motion of the hellish machine ceased and I beheld it drawn up, by some invisible force, through the ceiling. This was a lesson which I took desperately to heart. My every motion was undoubtedly watched. Free!—I had but escaped death in one form of agony, to be delivered unto worse than death in some other. With that thought I rolled my eyes nervously around on the barriers of iron that hemmed me in. Something unusual—some change which, at first, I could not appreciate distinctly—it was obvious, had taken place in the apartment. For many minutes of a dreamy and trembling abstraction, I busied myself in vain, unconnected conjecture. During this period, I became aware, for the first time, of the origin of the sulphurous light which illumined the cell. It proceeded from a fissure, about half an inch in width, extending entirely around the prison at the base of the walls, which thus appeared, and were, completely separated from the floor. I endeavored, but of course in vain, to look through the aperture.

As I arose from the attempt, the mystery of the alteration in the chamber broke at once upon my understanding. I have observed that, although the outlines of the figures upon the walls were sufficiently distinct, yet the colors seemed blurred and indefinite. These colors had now assumed, and were momentarily assuming, a startling and most intense brilliancy, that gave to the spectral and fiendish portraitures an aspect that might have thrilled even firmer nerves than my own. Demon eyes, of a wild and ghastly vivacity, glared upon me in a thousand directions, where none had been visible before, and gleamed with the lurid lustre of a fire that I could not force my imagination to regard as unreal.

Unreal!—Even while I breathed there came to my nostrils the breath of the vapour of heated iron! A suffocating odour pervaded the prison! A deeper glow settled each moment in the eyes that glared at my agonies! A richer tint of crimson diffused itself over the pictured horrors of blood. I panted! I gasped for breath! There could be no doubt of the design of my tormentors—oh! most unrelenting! oh! most demoniac of men! I shrank from the glowing metal to the centre of the cell. Amid the thought of the fiery destruction that impended, the idea of the coolness of the well came over my soul like balm. I rushed to its deadly brink. I threw my straining vision below. The glare from the enkindled roof illumined its inmost recesses. Yet, for a wild moment, did my spirit refuse to comprehend the meaning of what I saw. At length it forced—it wrestled its way into my soul—it burned itself in upon my shuddering reason. Oh! for a voice to speak!—oh! horror!—oh! any horror but this! With a shriek, I rushed from the margin, and buried my face in my hands—weeping bitterly.

The heat rapidly increased, and once again I looked up, shuddering as with a fit of the ague. There had been a second change in the cell—and now the change was obviously in the form. As before, it was in vain that I, at first, endeavoured to appreciate or understand what was taking place. But not long was I left in doubt. The Inquisitorial vengeance had been hurried by my two-fold escape, and there was to be no more dallying with the King of Terrors. The room had been square. I saw that two of its iron angles were now acute—two, consequently, obtuse. The fearful difference quickly increased with a low rumbling or moaning sound. In an instant the apartment had shifted its form into that of a lozenge. But the alteration stopped not here—I neither hoped nor desired it to stop. I could have clasped the red walls to my bosom as a garment of eternal peace. "Death," I said, "any death but that of the pit!" Fool! might I have not known that into the pit it was the object of the burning iron to urge me? Could I resist its glow? or, if even that, could I withstand its pressure? And now, flatter and flatter grew the lozenge, with a rapidity that left me no time for contemplation. Its centre, and of course, its greatest width, came just over the yawning gulf. I shrank back—but the closing walls pressed me resistlessly onward. At length for my seared and writhing body there was no longer an inch of foothold on the firm floor of the prison. I struggled no more, but the agony of my soul found vent in one loud, long, and final scream of despair. I felt that I tottered upon the brink—I averted my eyes—

There was a discordant hum of human voices! There was a loud blast as of many trumpets! There was a harsh grating as of a thousand thunders! The fiery walls rushed back! An outstretched arm caught my own as I fell, fainting, into the abyss. It was that of General Lasalle. The French army had entered Toledo. The Inquisition was in the hands of its enemies.

6

THE GREATEST ESCAPE: A TRUE AMERICAN CIVIL WAR ADVENTURE

BY DOUGLAS MILLER

Interesting news cannot grow stale; time cannot destroy that interest;
it cannot even fade it; the eye-witness's narrative which stirs the heart
to-day, will as surely and as profoundly stir it a thousand years hence.

—Mark Twain, autobiography

In 1893, Chicago became the center of the world. In an era of train travel, millions rode the iron horse to the city, journeying for days at a time so they could experience the great American World Fair. They went to be thrilled by the latest advancements in science and art, to witness the mechanical marvels they'd only read about, and to see if Americans could top the marvelous Paris World Exposition, which four years earlier had premiered the Eiffel Tower.

Many of America's finest architects had worked to create a brilliant "White City," with entries from around the world. The Chicago Fair was an enormous success, exposing patrons to an amazing range of inventions—from the movie theater to the Ferris wheel, which many patriotic Americans thought grander than Eiffel's tower. The splendor and massed humanity, richly described in Erik Larson's book, *The Devil in the White City*, still linger in the collective memory of Midwestern America.

One of the city's most popular attractions, not part of the fair but erected near to the fairgrounds, was the Libby Prison Civil War Museum. In a city crammed with curious exhibitions in unusual buildings, this museum was perhaps the most curious of all.

A massive brick-and-stone structure, Libby had actually been brought to Chicago from its home in Richmond, Virginia, some eight hundred miles away. Decades earlier, it had been constructed as a tobacco warehouse. During America's Civil War, the Confederate states chose Richmond for their capital city, and they converted the warehouse into a prison for Union officers. In the fourth year of the war, Union officers confined at Libby made the building world famous by staging the greatest prison escape in US history.

In 1888, almost 25 years after the war, a group of entrepreneurs bought the old building with the audacious goal of moving it to the city of Chicago. Thousands of bricks and beams were disassembled and carefully labeled. The totality was massive enough to fill 132 rail cars, each of which could haul 20 tons. The Chesapeake and Ohio Railroad won the high-profile contract, and was greatly embarrassed when their train wrecked near Maysville, Kentucky, scattering the contents along the right of way. But everything was carefully collected, reloaded, and safely delivered to the Windy City.

The four stories of Libby Prison were reconstructed on Wabash Avenue between Fourteenth and Sixteenth Streets and ringed with a massive stone wall, which gave it the aspect of a giant castle. Some $200,000—a veritable fortune in those days—had been spent by the time the museum opened in December 1889.

Flyers, pamphlets, and newspaper advertisements quickly followed. *"Attention! No Stranger Should Leave Chicago without visiting Libby Prison, the Great National War Museum,"* said one. The famous chaplain C. C. McCabe, who had almost died of disease and vermin infestation while imprisoned there, proclaimed that he had seen the Libby exhibit in Chicago, *"and pronounces it the grandest and most instructive museum in the world."*

The new museum was filled floor to ceiling, in the cluttered Victorian style of the day, with photographs, documents, oil paintings, and a sprawling collection of the war's remains: cannons and cutlasses, Confederate postage stamps and newspapers printed on wallpaper, military proclamations and recruiting posters, Jefferson Davis's love letters to his wife, and—from Appomattox—the very table on which Grant and Lee had signed the surrender. Also on display were ragged battle flags, tiny bone scrimshaws carved by POWs, and a collection of what were described in the museum catalog as *"War Logs: the collection of tree stumps in this room, filled with shot and shell, is the finest in existence."*

The Rebel surrender at Appomattox, less than three decades in the past, was within easy memory; many visitors who paid the fifty-cent admission fee (children twenty-five cents) had a personal connection to the war. For long after the fair had closed, the Libby Museum continued to pack in the crowds that came to see one of the Civil War's most famous locales—a battlefield all its own.

The most popular part of the exhibit, the one everybody wanted to experience, lay deep in the dark cellar of the old building. During the war, this dank space contained the rooms that served as punishment dungeons for men unfortunate enough to cross Rebel authorities. Those windowless rooms, in their day, had been suffused with the foulest of human and animal odors. One of the basement chambers had been so disgustingly filthy that imprisoned officers had tagged it with the nickname Rat Hell. In the new museum, of course, these rooms were so clean that the most prim and proper ladies and gentlemen would gladly visit them. And for an extra twenty-five cents, visitors could see that monument to human perseverance, the "Great Yankee Hole." Many thousands of people poked their heads into the entrance of the tunnel that had led 109 Union officers out of this "Rebel Bastille" in February of 1864.

The men who had actually entered that hole, and had made the difficult passage through the tunnel that led from it, were then pursued by Confederate hunters across fifty miles of freezing swamps;

without food or warm clothing or maps, they passed through a series of extreme trials and adventures—none of which the exhibit could more than hint at. Along their perilous journey three decades earlier, many of the Union officers had been helped by slaves and members of the "Union Underground," all of whom risked their lives by sheltering and shepherding the escaping Yankees.

Since Libby had been one of the first prisons established by the Confederacy, its worsening conditions were the subject of anger and consternation throughout the war. And as the Rebels had taken care to place the vaunted prison smack in the center of their capital city, it naturally became a focus of strong emotions on both sides.

So when more than a hundred Union officers vanished from the Confederacy's "escape-proof" building—and when the escape played out over the following weeks in newspapers North and South—the public was riveted. Each day brought new stories and revised numbers of officers escaped or recaptured. In a Civil War of mass slaughter, where tens of thousands of young men were expected to stand in rows and shoot each other to pieces, here was an uplifting tale in which ingenuity, perseverance, initiative, pluck, and luck had won the day. Brutally imprisoned, completely on their own, facing a slow death from starvation or disease, the young men in Libby had stood up and prevailed.

The tale of Libby Prison soon grew even more popular, thanks to the POWs themselves. Officers of the Union Army could read and write. And write they did. The more famous the escape became, the more the escapees wrote about it. The first accounts were published within months of the event. They continued to come out for decades—and for long after the Libby exhibit in Chicago had closed.

These prisoner memoirs were published with provocative titles like "Forgotten in the Black Hole," "What I Saw and Suffered in Rebel

Prisons," "The POW and How Treated," "A Thrilling History of the Famous Tunnel Escape from Libby Prison"—to the more leisurely and Victorian, "Extracts From My Diary and My Experiences while Boarding with Jeff Davis in Three of his Notorious Hotels."

These young Yankee officers wrote well and clearly, even though many of them modestly started their tales with "I'm not a writer but . . ." Americans were more literate back then, and even young men like these—most in their twenties—had plenty of writing experience, along with a vocabulary broad enough to include words like "cerements," "adamantine," "fugacious," "renitent," or "unpomatumed."

Their histories were very personal, with strong points of view. Many of the men, particularly those whose accounts appeared immediately, were furious at the treatment they'd received at the hands of the Rebels. As with most military memoirs, those written decades after the fact carried a mellower tone. Still expressing anger, they had been tempered by time and by the reconciliation the entire country was experiencing.

These first-person accounts were as diverse as the men who made up the Union officer corps. Some were only a few pages long; some were entire books filled with unique illustrations; some were from lectures; some were written days after the fact, while others weren't recorded until a half-century later. One memoir was written in German. Another was written by a future hero of the Cuban Revolution; another by a Sardinian immigrant who would become the first head of New York's Metropolitan Museum of Art; another by a Romanian soldier of fortune who had served with Garibaldi; and another by a POW chaplain who would carve out a lifelong career on the Chautauqua circuit by delivering, again and again, his one-of-a-kind sermon on "The Bright Side of Life in Libby."

What follows in this book is the story of the Libby Prison escape and its aftermath, truer than it's ever been told. The story is based on primary sources: the four dozen eyewitness accounts that, along with more than forty historic illustrations, took more than two decades to locate. The POWs who went through the tunnel considered it a supreme trial; for most, it was the greatest event of their lives. Their personal stories are front and center in this volume, each memoir adding a unique point of view about the escape and about the minds of Americans in 1864.

These personal accounts, in effect, are interviews with people who are speaking to us direct from the nineteenth century. These eyewitnesses were personal, passionate, funny, and often very sarcastic. The quotes have sometimes been shortened, because writers of that time were notably long-winded; and the spelling of names has been made uniform. Otherwise, original texts are unaltered; spelling and phrasing have been left intact, including racial language and various attempts at dialects and swearing. For the first time, a century and a half after the events, all the Libby memoirs are together in one place.

On April 4, 1865, one day after Richmond fell to the Union Army and ten days before he was assassinated, President Lincoln arrived to tour the fire-ravaged Rebel capital. One of the first sites he stopped at was Libby Prison. A boisterous crowd of soldiers and ex-slaves cheered, *"We'll tear it down"*—to which Lincoln replied, *"No, leave it as a monument."*

The American Civil War was the largest, most destructive conflict of its age. It was the greatest war in the Western Hemisphere. It was the most important event in the history of the United States. Its key triggers of race, states' rights, and militarism may have evolved, but they still define us. More than any event since the Revolution, the Civil

War made America what it is today. And the Libby Prison escape is one of its pivotal stories, as well as one of its greatest adventures.

The excerpt from *The Greatest Escape: A True American Civil War Adventure*, by Douglas Miller, continues with the book's chapter "First Night," describing the fates of the first escapees.

Rose and Hamilton, as instigators of the escape, were first through the tunnel. The hope was for pairs and trios of POWs to stick together and help each other along the way.

However, as Hamilton recorded,

> We walked two squares and then turned. Here we passed a hospital guard who insisted upon knowing where Rose was from. Not receiving satisfactory replies, Colonel [Rose] was taken to the chief officer of the guard, where he must have made some clever explanations, for he was away again in half an hour. In the meantime I came to the conclusion that the quarters were too close for me, and I trudged on alone.

Just minutes into their journey the two were already broken up and on their own. Rose remembered,

> Hamilton turned back and we became separated. I did not see him again for several months.
>
> No plan had been arranged to be pursued after we left prison. It was expected of each man to take care of himself and be governed by circumstances.

It might seem like an unlikely recipe for success, but not making specific escape plans actually worked in the prisoners' favor. The more than 100 men who passed through Richmond that night would have caused suspicion if they had gathered together or followed the same route. As it happened, every escaping man had to rely entirely on his own wits to get him through whatever he faced. The anarchy of their situation favored the POWs.

Lt. Wells, for example, knew little more than the direction he wanted to go.

I slipped out and walked eastward on Canal Street. I had no fixed plan for getting out of the city, but was guided wholly by impulse and by circumstances.

The Federal uniform and overcoat I wore was rather an advantage than otherwise, for the Confederate soldiers had appropriated clothing sent by our government and were then commonly wearing our overcoats on the streets.

Many of the POWs did not have Union uniforms, but instead wore civilian clothes they had received in their boxes shipped from home. Richmond was a crowded boomtown full of strangers, which also worked to the prisoners' advantage. In a close-knit city the POWs might have stood out and been spotted, but the Rebel capital was already full of scrawny young men wearing all manner of ragged uniforms in every state of disrepair.

It was a crisp, clear night. Any escaping officer could orient himself by the North Star. Everyone knew that 50 miles to the east were the front lines of the Union Army.

Young Lt. Earle was one of the first out, at around eight o'clock. It was still early evening. He strode boldly down one of the busiest thoroughfares in the city.

We passed out and walked slowly and deliberately—in full view of the guards, remember—but, assuming the manners of those walking in

the streets who had a right to do so. This was one of the most danger-
ous points we passed during the escape, and in many respects the most
wonderful. For the first time we were out of the range of the guards'
muskets. Of course we took a long breath.

We came to Cary Street, which was brilliantly lighted, and many
of the shops were still open. We observed a group of soldiers walking
in front of us, talking and laughing. We mingled freely with them,
talking to ourselves on subjects similar to those they were discuss-
ing. We avoided coming into direct contact with them, however, and
gradually as we approached the outskirts of the city, allowed them to
pass us, until at last we found ourselves about one mile to the east of
Richmond.

Cols. Hobart and West also decided the safest course was to go
straight down the main streets of the city, all the while working their
own special ruse.

My face being very pale and my beard long, clinging to the arm of Col.
West, I assumed the part of a decrepit old man who seemed to be badly
affected with a consumptive cough. In this manner we passed through
the glaring gaslights and the crowded streets without creating a suspi-
cion. We met the police, squads of soldiers, and many others who gave
me a sympathizing look and stepped aside. Approaching the suburbs
we retreated into a ravine which allowed us to leave the city.

Obviously, pretending to have a dreaded, communicable disease
was an effective disguise.

Capt. Johnston was ecstatic just to be out of Rat Hell for the first
time in days. Despite his worries, fortune was with him and he made
quick progress.

As my comrade and myself were passing through the city, two ladies who were standing at the gate of a house, observed us; one of them remarked to the other that we looked like Yankees. We did not stop to undeceive them, and met with no further trouble until the city limits were passed.

Men continued to flow out of the prison all night long. Lt. Moran, who had fought so hard to get down into Rat Hell and through the tunnel, had to walk the city after midnight when few others were about.

We moved quickly, but with great caution, for we knew that the provost guard compelled every one on the streets to exhibit the proper pass. In spite of care we found ourselves almost in the hands of the patrol several times. After repeated narrow escapes we turned a corner, and before we had a chance to exchange a word, a dozen Confederates, without arms, passed us without a suspicion that we were escaping Yankees. Grateful for our good fortune we moved rapidly forward. Dogs rushed at us from every house and set up a hideous howl.

Col. McCreery remembered how he and his partner "locked arms and marched out into the street under the archway near which was burning a bright gaslight. At first we took to the center of the street, but gaining confidence we ventured upon the sidewalk. We had not proceeded far when we were ordered by a sentinel to halt, and in reply to his interrogatory, 'Who goes there?' I answered, 'We are citizens going home,' to which he replied, 'Take the middle of the street! You know no one can walk on this yer' sidewalk in front of this yer' hospital after dark.' We were in hearty accord with the sentinel, and taking the middle of the street passed the hospital without further annoyance."

Col. Abel Streight and three companions almost came to disaster that first night. The plan was for them to shelter at Elizabeth Van Lew's mansion, then move to a safe house until things calmed down. But communications had failed and Van Lew did not receive information about the actual time of the escape. On the night of the 9th she had donned a disguise of rough clothing and left home to spend the night with her brother, a Rebel deserter who was also trying to get out of Richmond.

The next morning her servant arrived to bring her back to the mansion.

> As soon as he called, he said that there was great trouble and excitement; that many prisoners had escaped during the night, and that some had come to his door & begged to come in, but he was afraid they were not prisoners, only people in disguise to betray us & would not let them in.
>
> We knew there was to be an exit, had been told to prepare & had one of our parlors—had dark blankets nailed up at the windows and the gas had been kept burning in it very low. We were so ready for them, beds prepared in there. I returned home, after going as quickly as I could, in despair.

Luckily the POWs found a spot to hide through the night. Next day they were connected with a Mrs. Green, who led them to the humble home of fellow Unionist Mrs. Rice. Though Mrs. Rice was in poor health she treated her guests royally; they stayed a week, waiting for the Rebels to stop searching for POWs.

The rest of the escapees hoped to get well out of Richmond before dawn. They knew it would be extremely difficult to travel in daylight and not be noticed. Lt. Fales and his two companions had just reached the edge of the city when they had a risky encounter.

We heard the jingling of sabers, indicating that a small force of cavalry was coming towards us, and jumping over the fence, we suddenly came face to face upon a man who was out with a lantern getting a pail of water. This peaceful citizen was frightened, and in tremulous tones said: "What is the matter; what are you running for?" We replied that we were going to our regiments out at the forts, and passed on without stopping to explain further.

The cavalry having passed by towards the city, we returned to the road, and just as I jumped over the fence, four more cavalrymen came riding round the corner, and my comrades started back on the run. The enemy were too near for me to think of running, so I stood still, and on coming up, one of the soldiers asked: "Where are you going?" I replied: "Out to my regiment." Then he said: "What are those other fellows running for?" I gave some reply, exactly what, I do not now recollect, but the idea was, that they were absent from their regiments without permission. This satisfied the cavalrymen and they passed on without further conversation, greatly to my relief, for if they had asked me what regiment I belonged to, where the regiment was stationed, and other details, I should have been in a very dangerous situation.

It was logical for the Confederates to believe that these ragtag men were their own soldiers hustling back after a harmless sojourn in the big city. The cavalrymen probably did the same thing on occasion.

Lt. Wallber came out of the tunnel at 2 a.m. The city had quieted considerably and the gaslights had been turned off. He and his companion decided, because it was so late, to avoid the main streets.

A few steps away, a sentry called "Post number six—all well." He turned his back on me and I ducked around the corner to freedom.

Free, rid of the shackles that had held us so long, we breathed deep drafts of night air and shouted: "Thank God, Free at last!" From the bottom of our hearts we resolved to die rather than return to that dungeon. "Out of this hellhole as fast as possible to the land of freedom!"—and away we went double quick. We jumped fences, crashed across gardens, raced down boulevards, hustled through alleys, and startled dogs that barked at us.

Evading Rebel patrols, the pair got to the edge of the city without incident and found a railroad track that led east.

Briskly we followed it in single file. We had not gone far when a nearby hiss stopped us. We called out. A pair of comrades appeared beside us. They too had just escaped. We exchanged greetings and resumed the march along the railroad. At daybreak we took shelter in a piney woods.

The next barrier to get through was the elaborate system of defensive earthworks that surrounded Richmond. These interlocking fortifications were a formidable maze of ditches, ramparts, mines, trenches, bombproofs, and large siege guns. They had been constructed, on and off, throughout the war and formed an in-depth system so impressive that the Union never dared attack it.

However, with the Confederacy suffering a serious manpower shortage, and with no sizeable Yankee forces anywhere near Richmond, only a thin line of pickets was posted to watch over the trenches. These men were meant to form the first warning line against any attack from outside the Rebel capital; they were not on the lookout for individual Union prisoners escaping from inside the city.

"We made our way over numberless rifle pits, huge earthworks, tangled brush and fallen trees that would have proved a bloody path to an assault column," wrote Lt. Moran about his delicate passage through the trenches.

A dozen times we came within an ace of walking into the hands of guards. Having passed the city limits and the line of works successfully, our spirits rose in spite of empty stomachs and shivering limbs. The first gray streaks of day appear[ed] in the East as we saw ahead a number of small fires, and as they seemed to be at a uniform distance we concluded we had reached the outer line of pickets.

We saw no advantage in going to the right or left, hence we voted to attempt a passage in our immediate front. We went forward to within a hundred yards of the nearest post, and saw five armed Confederates. Their faces were to the fire and their backs were to us.

We dropped upon our hands and knees, and crept in single file, toward the center of the intervening space. Most of the ground was nearly bare, and, as we crept along the frozen earth, the brittle brush cracked treacherously, while the blazing logs illuminated our perilous way. At every snapping branch we looked anxiously on both sides, resolved, if challenged, to take to our heels and run the gantlet. The Confederates were laughing and talking, their faces turned towards the genial fire.

Having passed the danger point, and well out of hearing, we rose to our feet, and giving three cheers (in pantomime), broke into a lively trot, with increasing hopes of success; for fortune thus far had singularly favored us.

We entered a swamp, thickly grown with a low underbrush that afforded the best available concealment. Selecting a spot at the base of a large oak tree well carpeted with leaves, we stretched our exhausted limbs and soon shivered ourselves to sleep.

After he had successfully talked his way out of a tight spot with Rebel cavalrymen, Lt. Fales was rejoined by the two comrades who had run away. Together the trio quietly passed by the forts and made their way into the open country beyond, which brought them to their next barrier—the swampy Chickahominy River.

We came to the Chickahominy, and started to go in search of a bridge or ford, but after going a short distance I saw a Rebel picket lying beside a few glowing coals, only twenty feet away. The sentinel had apparently been asleep and was just commencing to rise when we started on the run back to the spot where we first struck the river. The sentinel did not challenge us or shoot, but threw some fresh fuel on his fire and made it burn brightly, as if trying to discover by the light what had disturbed him.

Terrified of being recaptured, the men quickly stripped off their clothing, held it over their heads, and waded into the icy river. It was only about thirty yards wide at that point but deep enough that they had to swim.

Our teeth were chattering with cold when we reached the opposite shore, though when we plunged in we were wet with perspiration. We dressed rapidly and were about to move on, when I found I had left my haversack with all my rations on the opposite bank. I did not think it prudent to abandon my supplies, and stripping again, I went back across the river and recovered my rations, but paid dearly for them, finding myself thoroughly chilled through on my return.

After three trips across the river, Fales found he could not warm his body up, and this would cause troubles later. The trio of men found a dry spot at the roots of a large pine tree and tried to rest until daylight passed.

Capt. Johnston and his companion made it out of Richmond with little trouble, but then found themselves disoriented by the dark defenses surrounding the city. The city had been all bustle and gas-light, but now they were out where it was silent—and they felt the presence of Confederate troops in every direction. "We soon came to the Rebel camps, which stretched round a great portion of the city. We were excited, of course, and bewildered for this first hour, not knowing whether we were in the path of safety or danger. All at once I became perfectly composed and told my comrade to follow me and I would conduct him safe through."

The pair carefully passed between the picket posts, aided by a briskly blowing wind that loudly rustled the leaves. Moving rapidly, they crossed over four different lines of unmanned defenses. Once they passed the last line, they found open land on which the timber had been felled to provide clear fields of fire for Rebel artillery. "Among this timber was our hiding place the first day—all the safer, no doubt, for being within a few hundred yards of the Rebel guns. The weather was excessively cold and our pantaloons were frozen stiff up to our knees. We did not dare to make a fire so near to the Rebel camp."

The escape had started out almost perfectly. Only one of the 109 escapees was captured inside the city limits. The other 108 successfully made it out of Richmond, crossed the earthworks that surrounded the Rebel capital, and reached a hiding place in time for dawn.

The Confederates were still unaware that anything major had happened. The guards at Libby awoke to what they saw as another boring day.

7

MOUNTAIN MAN ESCAPE EPIC

BY LAMAR UNDERWOOD

Before covered wagons crossed the plains, carrying pioneer settlers who dreamed of the lands beyond the distant mountains . . .

Before cowboys drove herds of cattle, eating dust and shouting "yippee-ki-yay" . . .

Before prospectors panned remote mountain creeks for pay dirt . . .

Long before these epic events were notched as icons in the history of the frontier mountain West, men with special skills and burning desires made their way into the peaks—into the vast unknown where only the footprints of Native Americans had ever marked the passage of men. Today these early explorers are called "mountain men." Their adventures, on their own in the great untouched wilderness, with hostile Indians a constant danger, are the stuff of a gigantic mass of legends, literature, and film.

These were bearded, rough-hewn men, wearing greasy buckskins, carrying muzzle-loading rifles and toting packs containing what they called "possibles"—gear they might need—everything from flint and steel to bullets and a spare knife. They knew how to be at home in the wilds, capable of doing everything from following a set of elk tracks to building a shelter—or even a cabin. They talked funny, with expressions like "Waugh!" meaning delight or disgust; "went under" for dying; "rubbed out" for killed by Indians; and calling themselves "this coon," or "this child." Even though they traveled and hunted in groups at times, for protection from raids by Native tribes, they were essentially loners. They had turned their backs on civilization, left the settlements of other men as far behind them as possible. A life "loose and free's as ary animal," as novelist A. B. Guthrie put it in *The Big Sky*.

Such a life did not come without a price.

Hugh Glass is crawling again.

Out of the dusty pages of history, out of the visions created by legends, mountain man Hugh Glass has been restored to life. In a feature film as big and colorful as they come, the story of Hugh Glass unfolds before our very eyes. The Hugh Glass crawling through the wilderness on the screen is portrayed by actor Leonardo DiCaprio in the movie *The Revenant*, the biggest and most realistic mountain man movie since *Jeremiah Johnson*.

Just as happened in real life, back in 1823, Hugh Glass is literally crawling for survival. He is near death from the horrific wounds of a grizzly attack. The bear's claws have slashed his body like sword blades, and the beast has taken great bites into Glass's body, even his head. Glass is so far gone that his two mountain man companions have given him up for dead. Not only have they left him alone, one of them has helped himself to Glass's rifle and all his gear.

Hugh Glass is not dead. Neither is he "very much alive," as the expression goes, but he is able to crawl. This is exactly what he does, with hopes of somehow clinging to life and making his way to Fort Kiowa, some 200 miles distant on the Missouri River in what is now South Dakota. As he crawls, he is fueled by his desire to live and a raging need to take revenge on the men who have betrayed him.

The Revenant is based on the novel with the same title by Michael Punke, originally published in 2002 and reissued by Picador in 2015, to coincide with the film's premiere. As a self-confessed addict of everything "mountain man"—from books and films to TV reality shows—I have been hooked by the action, scope, and filmmaking splendor of this film. The obvious questions spring to mind: Is this movie as good as *Jeremiah Johnson*? Does it treat the Huge Glass legend fairly?

Since *revenant* is a word I've never used (or even heard) in my life, I had to hit the dictionary to learn that it means "one that returns after death or a long absence." The storytelling promise in those words has attracted other writers and filmmakers before it appealed to those who created *The Revenant*. Hugh Glass's epic crawl and fight for life and revenge inspired the novel *Lord Grizzly* by Frederick Manfred and the movie *Man in the Wilderness* (1971). A half-dozen or so nonfiction books are also devoted to the Hugh Glass saga.

My interest in mountain men has led me to write some magazine articles about them and to edit an entire book, *Tales of the Mountain Men* (Lyons Press, 2004). The latter included a chapter on Hugh Glass, featuring an excerpt from *Lord Grizzly*. *The Revenant* caused my interest in Hugh Glass to boil over with new enthusiasm. Even before I saw the film, I wanted to learn everything I could about its production. And I wanted to know more about the man himself.

The producers of *The Revenant* make no claim that the film is a "true story," one that actually happened just as shown. The subtitle says, "Inspired by True Events." Michael Punke gives readers the same instruction in the original novel. That's fair enough, because the details of Hugh Glass's early life are clouded with mystery. The events of the grizzly attack and its aftermath are well documented, however. Hugh Glass did survive his injuries in a trek of survival and revenge that are now part of frontier history.

Although "the crawl" is a high point in the Huge Glass drama, both in the movie and in his real life, Huge Glass was no tenderfoot. We know today that his background was a mixture of myths, exaggerations, and a few hard and proven facts. We know for sure that by the time he ran into the nightmare grizzly, Hugh Glass at forty-three was a veteran of Indian fights and had the hunting and trapping skills that made mountain men self-sufficient.

Despite the sketchy details of his youth, we are told Hugh Glass was born in Pennsylvania in 1780. Legends, unsubstantiated, of his early years include the colorful, folk-hero tale of being captured by privateers commanded by Jean Lafitte. He is said to have been forced into piracy for two years before escaping in 1819 in the area of what today is Galveston, Texas.

Glass and a fellow escapee were resourceful and lucky enough to survive a trek north, through hostile Indian country. But their luck ran out in what is now Kansas, when a band of Pawnees captured them. As Glass watched, they commenced their favorite form of torture on his friend, pushing tiny sticks of fat pine into his body, from the feet on up. When they set fire to the lower sticks, the flames spread rapidly and made the body into a human torch.

Glass talked his way out of this fate, it is said, by begging the chief to accept a gift that had gone undiscovered in his pockets. The rare package of cinnabar, which makes brilliant red paint, saved his life. He lived several years with the Pawnees, learning their skills of survival living on the land as an adopted son of the tribe. He no doubt fought alongside them against enemy tribes, although attacks on white men are not recorded. His life with the Pawnees ended in 1822 when he joined his chief on a journey to St. Louis to smoke a peace pipe with the superintendent of Indian Affairs, William Clark, of Lewis and Clark fame. Glass left the tribe here, a loner without any ties, his eyes still turned from his native Pennsylvania to the mountains of the Upper Missouri.

Whether or not that happened as described, we do know for certain that in 1823, in St. Louis, he saw this ad in the January 16 issue of the *Missouri Republican*:

FOR THE ROCKY MOUNTAINS

The subscribers wish to engage One Hundred MEN, to ascend the Missouri to the Rocky Mountains. There to be employed as Hunters. As a compensation to each man fit for such business, $200 Per Annum will be given for his services, as aforesaid. For particulars, apply to J. V. GARMIER or W. ASHLEY, at St. Louis. The expedition will set out for this place on or before the first of March next.

ASHLEY and HENRY

General William Ashley was the expedition's organizer and leader, and Captain Andrew Henry was in charge of the advance brigade. Ashley's "One Hundred MEN" comprised several names that would eventually include a Mountain Man Hall of Fame, including Jim Bridger, then just seventeen. Hugh Glass was also there.

In late August, the advance party was encamped on the Grand River, in what is present-day Perkins County, South Dakota, rerouting their path to the Upper Missouri by way of the Yellowstone. Earlier that summer, one of their groups had lost sixteen men in an attack by the Arikara (Ree) tribe. They had retaliated with a murderous raid on the Arikara in which they had been supported by troops from Fort Leavenworth and warriors from the Arikara's deadliest enemy, the Sioux. Captain Henry's unit was to keep pushing toward the Upper Missouri to open the fur trade, while waiting for a second expedition from General Ashley to rendezvous with them the following spring and bring out the furs.

On August 23, Hugh Glass was hunting, carrying his beloved and trusty Kentucky flintlock, an Anstadt .53 caliber, capable of throwing a ball two hundred yards. Hunting alone, the way he preferred, Glass suddenly came upon two grizzly bear cubs. He knew instantly he was in trouble. The sow would not be far away. His fears were confirmed about the same time he got his flintlock ready. He got off a shot before she charged, but it did little good. The great bear was on him in a slashing, crashing storm of fury.

Glass was unconscious when fellow hunters from the brigade found him beneath the dead bear. (While the trapper's single shot had been effective, it was too late to stop the charge.) One of the trappers described Glass as "tore nearly to peases [sic]." They patched him up as best they could and carried him in a travois for a couple of days before Captain Henry decided Glass could not be saved. He paid two men a bonus to stay behind with Glass while the main body pressed on. Young Jim Bridger and John Fitzgerald—the latter, twenty-three and a hothead bully—volunteered to wait for Glass to die. They were to bury him and then catch up with the main group.

After a day or so, Glass was still breathing, but certainly seemed on the edge of death. The two men staying with him rolled him in a buffalo robe and started digging a grave.

Then came an Indian attack.

Bridger and Fitzgerald bolted, grabbing Glass's rifle and bag of "possibles," including his knife, before they ran.

The two men caught up with the main brigade and told Captain Henry that Hugh Glass was dead and buried.

Of course, Hugh Glass was not dead. Eventually he began to crawl, eating roots and berries, literally clawing his way over the ground like an animal. His life was probably saved when he found a buffalo carcass from a wolf kill. Eventually he could stand, and he limped along, using a crutch he'd made from a stick. Onward he continued, with visions of killing Bridger and Fitzgerald aflame in his thoughts. His journey eventually put him among friendly Sioux who helped him get to Fort Kiowa.

I have no intention of spoiling the movie by revealing what happened to Hugh Glass after he reached Fort Kiowa. Everyone knows Jim Bridger went on to become a legendary mountain man himself. As for Glass, I can say that he went on to other battles with Indian tribes before leaving the mountains for the Southwest. Life on the Santa Fe Trail could not hold him, however, and he returned to the high-country Rockies. In the winter of 1833, Glass and a fellow trapper were ambushed by Arikara while crossing the ice of the frozen Yellowstone River. This time there was no miracle to save the life of Hugh Glass.

The movie that brings us new revelations of the Hugh Glass legend is a big one—in every way. It runs for 2 hours and 36 minutes. It's action-packed, with all the color, sounds, and atmosphere of the era, and is far and away the most significant mountain man movie in decades. That it's compared to *Jeremiah Johnson* is inevitable, but *The Revenant* stands tall in its own right. Playing Hugh Glass, Leonardo DiCaprio heads a big cast that includes Will Poulter as Jim Bridger and Tom Hardy as John Fitzgerald. Distributed by 20th Century Fox, the movie was a big-budget enterprise co-produced by five companies and directed by Alejandro González Iñárritu, Academy Award–winning director of *Birdman*. Nominated for twelve Oscars at the 88th Annual Academy Awards, including Best Picture, *The Revenant* won for Best Cinematography (Emmanuel Lubezki) and Best Actor (DiCaprio), and Iñárritu won Best Director for the second time. "When you see the film, you will see the scale of it," Iñárritu told Kim Masters in an interview for *The Hollywood Reporter*. "And you will say, Wow!"

Such Hollywood trade publications revealed the difficulties in filming *The Revenant*. Shot in Alberta and Argentina, the film's autumn setting was difficult to re-create in weather conditions that were sometimes too hot, and often too cold. While Iñárritu and Lubezki's decision to shoot only in natural light heightens the realism immensely, it was a tough taskmaster for filming schedules. In addition, Iñárritu refused to use computer-generated effects.

I already mentioned that I'm a mountain man junkie, eager for books, films, and whatever other artistic creations I can find to transport my mind and spirit to the time when such men roamed the mountains, "loose and free's as ary animal." This old coon's got a taste for it. We'll find beaver, one place or t'other. Waugh!

8

TO BUILD A FIRE

BY JACK LONDON

You are a prospector, swept up in the dream of acquiring riches in the Klondike Gold Rush of 1896–1899. Today you are hiking alone along the Yukon to reach a camp where your companions are waiting. You're not really alone, however. A husky, a malamute, is at your side, and is clearly showing signs of reluctance about this journey. The dog keeps holding back, and you fail to pay much attention to its behavior. Even without wind, the day is cold, colder perhaps than you have ever experienced in your second year in the Klondike. But you're dressed for it, and your hike is keeping you warm. Nonetheless, through its primal instincts, the dog knows something you do not: The cold is deeper and more forbidding than any it has ever known.

Day had broken cold and grey, exceedingly cold and grey, when the man turned aside from the main Yukon trail and climbed the high earth-bank, where a dim and little-travelled trail led eastward through the fat spruce timberland. It was a steep bank, and he paused for breath at the top, excusing the act to himself by looking at his watch. It was nine o'clock. There was no sun nor hint of sun, though there was not a cloud in the sky. It was a clear day, and yet there seemed an intangible pall over the face of things, a subtle gloom that made the day dark, and that was due to the absence of sun. This fact did not worry the man. He was used to the lack of sun. It had been days since he had seen the sun, and he knew that a few more days must pass before that cheerful orb, due south, would just peep above the sky-line and dip immediately from view.

The man flung a look back along the way he had come. The Yukon lay a mile wide and hidden under three feet of ice. On top of this ice were as many feet of snow. It was all pure white, rolling in gentle undulations where the ice-jams of the freeze-up had formed. North and south, as far as his eye could see, it was unbroken white, save for a dark hair-line that curved and twisted from around the spruce-covered island to the south, and that curved and twisted away into the north, where it disappeared behind another spruce-covered island. This dark hair-line was the trail—the main trail—that led south five hundred miles to the Chilcoot Pass, Dyea, and salt water; and that led north seventy miles to Dawson, and still on to the north a thousand miles to Nulato, and finally to St. Michael on the Bering Sea, a thousand miles and half a thousand more.

But all this—the mysterious, far-reaching hairline trail, the absence of sun from the sky, the tremendous cold, and the strangeness and weirdness of it all—made no impression on the man. It was not because he was long used to it. He was a new-comer in the land, a *chechaquo*, and this was his first winter. The trouble with him was that he was without imagination. He was quick and alert in the things of life, but only in the things, and not in the significances. Fifty degrees below zero meant eighty odd degrees of frost. Such fact impressed him as being cold and uncomfortable, and that was all. It did not lead him to meditate upon his frailty as a creature of temperature, and upon man's frailty in general, able only to live within certain narrow limits of heat and cold; and from there on it did not lead him to the conjectural field of immortality and man's place in the universe. Fifty degrees below zero stood for a bite of frost that hurt and that must be guarded against by the use of mittens, ear-flaps, warm moccasins, and thick socks. Fifty degrees below zero was to him just precisely fifty degrees below zero. That there should be anything more to it than that was a thought that never entered his head.

As he turned to go on, he spat speculatively. There was a sharp, explosive crackle that startled him. He spat again. And again, in the air, before it could fall to the snow, the spittle crackled. He knew that at fifty below spittle crackled on the snow, but this spittle had crackled in the air. Undoubtedly it was colder than fifty below—how much colder he did not know. But the temperature did not matter. He was bound for the old claim on the left fork of Henderson Creek, where the boys were already. They had come over across the divide from the Indian Creek country, while he had come the roundabout way to take a look at the possibilities of getting out logs in the spring from the islands in the Yukon. He would be in to camp by six o'clock; a bit after dark, it was true, but the boys would be there, a fire would be going, and a hot supper would be ready. As for lunch, he pressed his hand against the protruding bundle under his jacket. It was also under his shirt, wrapped up in a handkerchief and lying against the naked skin. It was the only way to keep the biscuits from freezing. He smiled agreeably to himself as he thought of those biscuits, each cut open and sopped in bacon grease, and each enclosing a generous slice of fried bacon.

He plunged in among the big spruce trees. The trail was faint. A foot of snow had fallen since the last sled had passed over, and he was glad he was without a sled, travelling light. In fact, he carried nothing but the lunch wrapped in the handkerchief. He was surprised, however, at the cold. It certainly was cold, he concluded, as he rubbed his numbed nose and cheek-bones with his mittened hand. He was a warm-whiskered man, but the hair on his face did not protect the high cheek-bones and the eager nose that thrust itself aggressively into the frosty air.

At the man's heels trotted a dog, a big native husky, the proper wolf-dog, grey-coated and without any visible or temperamental difference from its brother, the wild wolf. The animal was depressed by the tremendous cold. It knew that it was no time for travelling.

Its instinct told it a truer tale than was told to the man by the man's judgment. In reality, it was not merely colder than fifty below zero; it was colder than sixty below, than seventy below. It was seventy-five below zero. Since the freezing-point is thirty-two above zero, it meant that one hundred and seven degrees of frost obtained. The dog did not know anything about thermometers. Possibly in its brain there was no sharp consciousness of a condition of very cold such as was in the man's brain. But the brute had its instinct. It experienced a vague but menacing apprehension that subdued it and made it slink along at the man's heels, and that made it question eagerly every unwonted movement of the man as if expecting him to go into camp or to seek shelter somewhere and build a fire. The dog had learned fire, and it wanted fire, or else to burrow under the snow and cuddle its warmth away from the air.

The frozen moisture of its breathing had settled on its fur in a fine powder of frost, and especially were its jowls, muzzle, and eyelashes whitened by its crystalled breath. The man's red beard and moustache were likewise frosted, but more solidly, the deposit taking the form of ice and increasing with every warm, moist breath he exhaled. Also, the man was chewing tobacco, and the muzzle of ice held his lips so rigidly that he was unable to clear his chin when he expelled the juice. The result was that a crystal beard of the colour and solidity of amber was increasing its length on his chin. If he fell down it would shatter itself, like glass, into brittle fragments. But he did not mind the appendage. It was the penalty all tobacco-chewers paid in that country, and he had been out before in two cold snaps. They had not been so cold as this, he knew, but by the spirit thermometer at Sixty Mile he knew they had been registered at fifty below and at fifty-five.

He held on through the level stretch of woods for several miles, crossed a wide flat of huge tussocks, and dropped down a bank to the frozen bed of a small stream. This was Henderson Creek, and he knew he was ten miles from the forks. He looked at his watch. It was ten o'clock. He was making four miles an hour, and he calculated that he would arrive at the forks at half-past twelve. He decided to celebrate that event by eating his lunch there.

The dog dropped in again at his heels, with a tail drooping discouragement, as the man swung along the creek-bed. The furrow of the old sled-trail was plainly visible, but a dozen inches of snow covered the marks of the last runners. In a month no man had come up or down that silent creek. The man held steadily on. He was not much given to thinking, and just then particularly he had nothing to think about save that he would eat lunch at the forks and that at six o'clock he would be in camp with the boys. There was nobody to talk to and, had there been, speech would have been impossible because of the ice-muzzle on his mouth. So he continued monotonously to chew tobacco and to increase the length of his amber beard.

Once in a while the thought reiterated itself that it was very cold and that he had never experienced such cold. As he walked along he rubbed his cheek-bones and nose with the back of his mittened hand. He did this automatically, now and again changing hands. But rub as he would, the instant he stopped his cheek-bones went numb, and the following instant the end of his nose went numb. He was sure to frost his cheeks; he knew that, and experienced a pang of regret that he had not devised a nose-strap of the sort Bud wore in cold snaps. Such a strap passed across the cheeks, as well, and saved them. But it didn't matter much, after all. What were frosted cheeks? A bit painful, that was all; they were never serious.

Empty as the man's mind was of thoughts, he was keenly observant, and he noticed the changes in the creek, the curves and bends and timber-jams, and always he sharply noted where he placed his feet.

Once, coming around a bend, he shied abruptly, like a startled horse, curved away from the place where he had been walking, and retreated several paces back along the trail. The creek he knew was frozen clear to the bottom—no creek could contain water in that arctic winter— but he knew also that there were springs that bubbled out from the hillsides and ran along under the snow and on top of the ice of the creek. He knew that the coldest snaps never froze these springs, and he knew likewise their danger. They were traps. They hid pools of water under the snow that might be three inches deep, or three feet. Sometimes a skin of ice half an inch thick covered them, and in turn was covered by the snow. Sometimes there were alternate layers of water and ice-skin, so that when one broke through he kept on breaking through for a while, sometimes wetting himself to the waist.

That was why he had shied in such panic. He had felt the give under his feet and heard the crackle of a snow-hidden ice-skin. And to get his feet wet in such a temperature meant trouble and danger. At the very least it meant delay, for he would be forced to stop and build a fire, and under its protection to bare his feet while he dried his socks and moccasins. He stood and studied the creek-bed and its banks, and decided that the flow of water came from the right. He reflected awhile, rubbing his nose and cheeks, then skirted to the left, stepping gingerly and testing the footing for each step. Once clear of the danger, he took a fresh chew of tobacco and swung along at his four-mile gait.

In the course of the next two hours he came upon several similar traps. Usually the snow above the hidden pools had a sunken, candied appearance that advertised the danger. Once again, however, he had a close call; and once, suspecting danger, he compelled the dog to go on in front. The dog did not want to go. It hung back until the man shoved it forward, and then it went quickly across the white, unbroken surface. Suddenly it broke through, floundered to one side, and got away to firmer footing.

It had wet its forefeet and legs, and almost immediately the water that clung to it turned to ice. It made quick efforts to lick the ice off its legs, then dropped down in the snow and began to bite out the ice that had formed between the toes. This was a matter of instinct. To permit the ice to remain would mean sore feet. It did not know this. It merely obeyed the mysterious prompting that arose from the deep crypts of its being. But the man knew, having achieved a judgment on the subject, and he removed the mitten from his right hand and helped tear out the ice-particles. He did not expose his fingers more than a minute, and was astonished at the swift numbness that smote them. It certainly was cold. He pulled on the mitten hastily, and beat the hand savagely across his chest.

At twelve o'clock the day was at its brightest. Yet the sun was too far south on its winter journey to clear the horizon. The bulge of the earth intervened between it and Henderson Creek, where the man walked under a clear sky at noon and cast no shadow. At half-past twelve, to the minute, he arrived at the forks of the creek. He was pleased at the speed he had made. If he kept it up, he would certainly be with the boys by six. He unbuttoned his jacket and shirt and drew forth his lunch. The action consumed no more than a quarter of a minute, yet in that brief moment the numbness laid hold of the exposed fingers. He did not put the mitten on, but, instead, struck the fingers a dozen sharp smashes against his leg. Then he sat down on a snow-covered log to eat. The sting that followed upon the striking of his fingers against his leg ceased so quickly that he was startled; he had had no chance to take a bite of biscuit. He struck the fingers repeatedly and returned them to the mitten, baring the other hand for the purpose of eating. He tried to take a mouthful, but the ice-muzzle prevented. He had forgotten to build a fire and thaw out. He chuckled at his foolishness, and as he chuckled he noted the numbness creeping into the exposed fingers. Also, he noted that the stinging which had first come to his toes when he sat down was already passing away. He wondered whether the toes were warm or numbed. He moved them inside the moccasins and decided that they were numbed.

He pulled the mitten on hurriedly and stood up. He was a bit frightened. He stamped up and down until the stinging returned into the feet. It certainly was cold, was his thought. That man from Sulphur Creek had spoken the truth when telling how cold it sometimes got in the country. And he had laughed at him at the time! That showed one must not be too sure of things. There was no mistake about it, it was cold. He strode up and down, stamping his feet and threshing his arms, until reassured by the returning warmth. Then he got out matches and proceeded to make a fire. From the undergrowth, where high water of the previous spring had lodged a supply of seasoned twigs, he got his firewood. Working carefully from a small beginning, he soon had a roaring fire, over which he thawed the ice from his face and in the protection of which he ate his biscuits. For the moment the cold of space was outwitted. The dog took satisfaction in the fire, stretching out close enough for warmth and far enough away to escape being singed.

When the man had finished, he filled his pipe and took his comfortable time over a smoke. Then he pulled on his mittens, settled the ear-flaps of his cap firmly about his ears, and took the creek trail up the left fork. The dog was disappointed and yearned back toward the fire. This man did not know cold. Possibly all the generations of his ancestry had been ignorant of cold, of real cold, of cold one hundred and seven degrees below freezing-point. But the dog knew; all its ancestry knew, and it had inherited the knowledge. And it knew that it was not good to walk abroad in such fearful cold. It was the time to lie snug in a hole in the snow and wait for a curtain of cloud to be drawn across the face of outer space whence this cold came. On the other hand, there was keen intimacy between the dog and the man. The one was the toil-slave of the other, and the only caresses it had ever received were the caresses of the whip-lash and of harsh and menacing throat-sounds that threatened the whip-lash. So the dog made no effort to communicate its apprehension to the man. It was not concerned in the welfare of the man; it was for its own sake that it yearned back toward the fire. But the man whistled, and spoke to it with the sound of whip-lashes, and the dog swung in at the man's heels and followed after.

The man took a chew of tobacco and proceeded to start a new amber beard. Also, his moist breath quickly powdered with white his moustache, eyebrows, and lashes. There did not seem to be so many springs on the left fork of the Henderson, and for half an hour the man saw no signs of any. And then it happened. At a place where there were no signs, where the soft, unbroken snow seemed to advertise solidity beneath, the man broke through. It was not deep. He wetted himself half-way to the knees before he floundered out to the firm crust.

He was angry, and cursed his luck aloud. He had hoped to get into camp with the boys at six o'clock, and this would delay him an hour, for he would have to build a fire and dry out his foot-gear. This was imperative at that low temperature—he knew that much; and he turned aside to the bank, which he climbed. On top, tangled in the underbrush about the trunks of several small spruce trees, was a high-water deposit of dry firewood—sticks and twigs principally, but also larger portions of seasoned branches and fine, dry, last-year's grasses. He threw down several large pieces on top of the snow. This served for a foundation and prevented the young flame from drowning itself in the snow it otherwise would melt. The flame he got by touching a match to a small shred of birch-bark that he took from his pocket. This burned even more readily than paper. Placing it on the foundation, he fed the young flame with wisps of dry grass and with the tiniest dry twigs.

He worked slowly and carefully, keenly aware of his danger. Gradually, as the flame grew stronger, he increased the size of the twigs with which he fed it. He squatted in the snow, pulling the twigs out from their entanglement in the brush and feeding directly to the flame. He knew there must be no failure. When it is seventy-five below zero, a man must not fail in his first attempt to build a fire— that is, if his feet are wet. If his feet are dry, and he fails, he can run along the trail for half a mile and restore his circulation. But the circulation of wet and freezing feet cannot be restored by running when it is seventy-five below. No matter how fast he runs, the wet feet will freeze the harder.

All this the man knew. The old-timer on Sulphur Creek had told him about it the previous fall, and now he was appreciating the advice. Already all sensation had gone out of his feet. To build the fire he had been forced to remove his mittens, and the fingers had quickly gone numb. His pace of four miles an hour had kept his heart pumping blood to the surface of his body and to all the extremities. But the instant he stopped, the action of the pump eased down. The cold of space smote the unprotected tip of the planet, and he, being on that unprotected tip, received the full force of the blow. The blood of his body recoiled before it. The blood was alive, like the dog, and like the dog it wanted to hide away and cover itself up from the fearful cold. So long as he walked four miles an hour, he pumped that blood, willy-nilly, to the surface; but now it ebbed away and sank down into the recesses of his body. The extremities were the first to feel its absence. His wet feet froze the faster, and his exposed fingers numbed the faster, though they had not yet begun to freeze. Nose and cheeks were already freezing, while the skin of all his body chilled as it lost its blood.

But he was safe. Toes and nose and cheeks would be only touched by the frost, for the fire was beginning to burn with strength. He was feeding it with twigs the size of his finger. In another minute he would be able to feed it with branches the size of his wrist, and then he could remove his wet foot-gear, and, while it dried, he could keep his naked feet warm by the fire, rubbing them at first, of course, with snow. The fire was a success. He was safe. He remembered the advice of the old-timer on Sulphur Creek, and smiled. The old-timer had been very serious in laying down the law that no man must travel alone in the Klondike after fifty below. Well, here he was; he had had the accident; he was alone; and he had saved himself. Those old-timers were rather womanish, some of them, he thought. All a man had to do was to keep his head, and he was all right. Any man who was a man could travel alone. But it was surprising, the rapidity with which his cheeks and nose were freezing. And he had not thought his fingers could go lifeless in so short a time. Lifeless they were, for he could scarcely make them move together to grip a twig, and they seemed remote from his body and from him. When he touched a twig, he had to look and see whether or not he had hold of it. The wires were pretty well down between him and his finger-ends.

All of which counted for little. There was the fire, snapping and crackling and promising life with every dancing flame. He started to untie his moccasins. They were coated with ice; the thick German socks were like sheaths of iron half-way to the knees; and the moccasin strings were like rods of steel all twisted and knotted as by some conflagration. For a moment he tugged with his numbed fingers, then, realizing the folly of it, he drew his sheath-knife.

But before he could cut the strings, it happened. It was his own fault or, rather, his mistake. He should not have built the fire under the spruce tree. He should have built it in the open. But it had been easier to pull the twigs from the brush and drop them directly on the fire. Now the tree under which he had done this carried a weight of snow on its boughs. No wind had blown for weeks, and each bough was fully freighted. Each time he had pulled a twig he had communicated a slight agitation to the tree—an imperceptible agitation, so far as he was concerned, but an agitation sufficient to bring about the disaster. High up in the tree one bough capsized its load of snow. This fell on the boughs beneath, capsizing them. This process continued, spreading out and involving the whole tree. It grew like an avalanche, and it descended without warning upon the man and the fire, and the fire was blotted out! Where it had burned was a mantle of fresh and disordered snow.

The man was shocked. It was as though he had just heard his own sentence of death. For a moment he sat and stared at the spot where the fire had been. Then he grew very calm. Perhaps the old-timer on Sulphur Creek was right. If he had only had a trail-mate he would have been in no danger now. The trail-mate could have built the fire. Well, it was up to him to build the fire over again, and this second time there must be no failure. Even if he succeeded, he would most likely lose some toes. His feet must be badly frozen by now, and there would be some time before the second fire was ready.

Such were his thoughts, but he did not sit and think them. He was busy all the time they were passing through his mind. He made a new foundation for a fire, this time in the open; where no treacherous tree could blot it out. Next, he gathered dry grasses and tiny twigs from the high-water flotsam. He could not bring his fingers together to pull them out, but he was able to gather them by the handful. In this way he got many rotten twigs and bits of green moss that were undesirable, but it was the best he could do. He worked methodically, even collecting an armful of the larger branches to be used later when the fire gathered strength. And all the while the dog sat and watched him, a certain yearning wistfulness in its eyes, for it looked upon him as the fire-provider, and the fire was slow in coming.

When all was ready, the man reached in his pocket for a second piece of birch-bark. He knew the bark was there, and, though he could not feel it with his fingers, he could hear its crisp rustling as he fumbled for it. Try as he would, he could not clutch hold of it. And all the time, in his consciousness, was the knowledge that each instant his feet were freezing. This thought tended to put him in a panic, but he fought against it and kept calm. He pulled on his mittens with his teeth, and threshed his arms back and forth, beating his hands with all his might against his sides. He did this sitting down, and he stood up to do it; and all the while the dog sat in the snow, its wolf-brush of a tail curled around warmly over its forefeet, its sharp wolf-ears pricked forward intently as it watched the man. And the man, as he beat and threshed with his arms and hands, felt a great surge of envy as he regarded the creature that was warm and secure in its natural covering.

After a time he was aware of the first far-away signals of sensation in his beaten fingers. The faint tingling grew stronger till it evolved into a stinging ache that was excruciating, but which the man hailed with satisfaction. He stripped the mitten from his right hand and fetched forth the birch-bark. The exposed fingers were quickly going numb again. Next he brought out his bunch of sulphur matches. But the tremendous cold had already driven the life out of his fingers. In his effort to separate one match from the others, the whole bunch fell in the snow. He tried to pick it out of the snow, but failed. The dead fingers could neither touch nor clutch. He was very careful. He drove the thought of his freezing feet, and nose, and cheeks, out of his mind, devoting his whole soul to the matches. He watched, using the sense of vision in place of that of touch, and when he saw his fingers on each side the bunch, he closed them—that is, he willed to close them, for the wires were drawn, and the fingers did not obey. He pulled the mitten on the right hand, and beat it fiercely against his knee. Then, with both mittened hands, he scooped the bunch of matches, along with much snow, into his lap. Yet he was no better off.

After some manipulation he managed to get the bunch between the heels of his mittened hands. In this fashion he carried it to his mouth. The ice crackled and snapped when by a violent effort he opened his mouth. He drew the lower jaw in, curled the upper lip out of the way, and scraped the bunch with his upper teeth in order to separate a match. He succeeded in getting one, which he dropped on his lap. He was no better off. He could not pick it up. Then he devised a way. He picked it up in his teeth and scratched it on his leg. Twenty times he scratched before he succeeded in lighting it. As it flamed he held it with his teeth to the birch-bark. But the burning brimstone went up his nostrils and into his lungs, causing him to cough spasmodically. The match fell into the snow and went out.

The old-timer on Sulphur Creek was right, he thought in the moment of controlled despair that ensued: after fifty below, a man should travel with a partner. He beat his hands, but failed in exciting any sensation. Suddenly he bared both hands, removing the mittens with his teeth. He caught the whole bunch between the heels of his hands. His arm-muscles not being frozen enabled him to press the hand-heels tightly against the matches. Then he scratched the bunch along his leg. It flared into flame, seventy sulphur matches at once! There was no wind to blow them out. He kept his head to one side to escape the strangling fumes, and held the blazing bunch to the birch-bark. As he so held it, he became aware of sensation in his hand. His flesh was burning. He could smell it. Deep down below the surface he could feel it. The sensation developed into pain that grew acute. And still he endured it, holding the flame of the matches clumsily to the bark that would not light readily because his own burning hands were in the way, absorbing most of the flame.

At last, when he could endure no more, he jerked his hands apart. The blazing matches fell sizzling into the snow, but the birch-bark was alight. He began laying dry grasses and the tiniest twigs on the flame. He could not pick and choose, for he had to lift the fuel between the heels of his hands. Small pieces of rotten wood and green moss clung to the twigs, and he bit them off as well as he could with his teeth. He cherished the flame carefully and awkwardly. It meant life, and it must not perish. The withdrawal of blood from the surface of his body now made him begin to shiver, and he grew more awkward. A large piece of green moss fell squarely on the little fire. He tried to poke it out with his fingers, but his shivering frame made him poke too far, and he disrupted the nucleus of the little fire, the burning grasses and tiny twigs separating and scattering. He tried to poke them together again, but in spite of the tenseness of the effort, his shivering got away with him, and the twigs were hopelessly scattered. Each twig gushed a puff of smoke and went out. The fire-provider had failed. As he looked apathetically about him, his eyes chanced on the dog, sitting across the ruins of the fire from him, in the snow, making restless, hunching movements, slightly lifting one forefoot and then the other, shifting its weight back and forth on them with wistful eagerness.

The sight of the dog put a wild idea into his head. He remembered the tale of the man, caught in a blizzard, who killed a steer and crawled inside the carcass, and so was saved. He would kill the dog and bury his hands in the warm body until the numbness went out of them. Then he could build another fire. He spoke to the dog, calling it to him; but in his voice was a strange note of fear that frightened the animal, who had never known the man to speak in such a way before. Something was the matter, and its suspicious nature sensed danger—it knew not what danger but somewhere, somehow, in its brain arose an apprehension of the man. It flattened its ears down at the sound of the man's voice, and its restless, hunching movements and the liftings and shiftings of its forefeet became more pronounced but it would not come to the man. He got on his hands and knees and crawled toward the dog. This unusual posture again excited suspicion, and the animal sidled mincingly away.

The man sat up in the snow for a moment and struggled for calmness. Then he pulled on his mittens, by means of his teeth, and got upon his feet. He glanced down at first in order to assure himself that he was really standing up, for the absence of sensation in his feet left him unrelated to the earth. His erect position in itself started to drive the webs of suspicion from the dog's mind; and when he spoke peremptorily, with the sound of whip-lashes in his voice, the dog rendered its customary allegiance and came to him. As it came within reaching distance, the man lost his control. His arms flashed out to the dog, and he experienced genuine surprise when he discovered that his hands could not clutch, that there was neither bend nor feeling in the fingers. He had forgotten for the moment that they were frozen and that they were freezing more and more. All this happened quickly, and before the animal could get away, he encircled its body with his arms. He sat down in the snow, and in this fashion held the dog, while it snarled and whined and struggled.

But it was all he could do, hold its body encircled in his arms and sit there. He realized that he could not kill the dog. There was no way to do it. With his helpless hands he could neither draw nor hold his sheath-knife nor throttle the animal. He released it, and it plunged wildly away, with tail between its legs, and still snarling. It halted forty feet away and surveyed him curiously, with ears sharply pricked forward. The man looked down at his hands in order to locate them, and found them hanging on the ends of his arms. It struck him as curious that one should have to use his eyes in order to find out where his hands were. He began threshing his arms back and forth, beating the mittened hands against his sides. He did this for five minutes, violently, and his heart pumped enough blood up to the surface to put a stop to his shivering. But no sensation was aroused in the hands. He had an impression that they hung like weights on the ends of his arms, but when he tried to run the impression down, he could not find it.

A certain fear of death, dull and oppressive, came to him. This fear quickly became poignant as he realized that it was no longer a mere matter of freezing his fingers and toes, or of losing his hands and feet, but that it was a matter of life and death with the chances against him. This threw him into a panic, and he turned and ran up the creek-bed along the old, dim trail. The dog joined in behind and kept up with him. He ran blindly, without intention, in fear such as he had never known in his life. Slowly, as he ploughed and floundered through the snow, he began to see things again—the banks of the creek, the old timber-jams, the leafless aspens, and the sky. The running made him feel better. He did not shiver. Maybe, if he ran on, his feet would thaw out; and, anyway, if he ran far enough, he would reach camp and the boys. Without doubt he would lose some fingers and toes and some of his face; but the boys would take care of him, and save the rest of him when he got there. And at the same time there was another thought in his mind that said he would never get to the camp and the boys; that it was too many miles away, that the freezing had too great a start on him, and that he would soon be stiff and dead. This thought he kept in the background and refused to consider. Sometimes it pushed itself forward and demanded to be heard, but he thrust it back and strove to think of other things.

It struck him as curious that he could run at all on feet so frozen that he could not feel them when they struck the earth and took the weight of his body. He seemed to himself to skim along above the surface and to have no connection with the earth. Somewhere he had once seen a winged Mercury, and he wondered if Mercury felt as he felt when skimming over the earth.

His theory of running until he reached camp and the boys had one flaw in it: he lacked the endurance. Several times he stumbled, and finally he tottered, crumpled up, and fell. When he tried to rise, he failed. He must sit and rest, he decided, and next time he would merely walk and keep on going. As he sat and regained his breath, he noted that he was feeling quite warm and comfortable. He was not shivering, and it even seemed that a warm glow had come to his chest and trunk. And yet, when he touched his nose or cheeks, there was no sensation. Running would not thaw them out. Nor would it thaw out his hands and feet. Then the thought came to him that the frozen portions of his body must be extending. He tried to keep this thought down, to forget it, to think of something else; he was aware of the panicky feeling that it caused, and he was afraid of the panic. But the thought asserted itself, and persisted, until it produced a vision of his body totally frozen. This was too much, and he made another wild run along the trail. Once he slowed down to a walk, but the thought of the freezing extending itself made him run again.

And all the time the dog ran with him, at his heels. When he fell down a second time, it curled its tail over its forefeet and sat in front of him, facing him, curiously eager and intent. The warmth and security of the animal angered him, and he cursed it till it flattened down its ears appeasingly. This time the shivering came more quickly upon the man. He was losing in his battle with the frost. It was creeping into his body from all sides. The thought of it drove him on, but he ran no more than a hundred feet, when he staggered and pitched headlong. It was his last panic. When he had recovered his breath and control, he sat up and entertained in his mind the conception of meeting death with dignity. However, the conception did not come to him in such terms. His idea of it was that he had been making a fool of himself, running around like a chicken with its head cut off—such was the simile that occurred to him. Well, he was bound to freeze anyway, and he might as well take it decently. With this new-found peace of mind came the first glimmerings of drowsiness. A good idea, he thought, to sleep off to death. It was like taking an anesthetic. Freezing was not so bad as people thought. There were lots worse ways to die.

He pictured the boys finding his body next day. Suddenly he found himself with them, coming along the trail and looking for himself. And, still with them, he came around a turn in the trail and found himself lying in the snow. He did not belong with himself any more, for even then he was out of himself, standing with the boys and looking at himself in the snow. It certainly was cold, was his thought. When he got back to the States he could tell the folks what real cold was. He drifted on from this to a vision of the old-timer on Sulphur Creek. He could see him quite clearly, warm and comfortable, and smoking a pipe.

"You were right, old hoss; you were right," the man mumbled to the old-timer of Sulphur Creek.

Then the man drowsed off into what seemed to him the most comfortable and satisfying sleep he had ever known. The dog sat facing him and waiting. The brief day drew to a close in a long, slow twilight. There were no signs of a fire to be made, and, besides, never in the dog's experience had it known a man to sit like that in the snow and make no fire. As the twilight drew on, its eager yearning for the fire mastered it, and with a great lifting and shifting of forefeet, it whined softly, then flattened its ears down in anticipation of being chided by the man. But the man remained silent. Later, the dog whined loudly. And still later it crept close to the man and caught the scent of death. This made the animal bristle and back away. A little longer it delayed, howling under the stars that leaped and danced and shone brightly in the cold sky. Then it turned and trotted up the trail in the direction of the camp it knew, where were the other food-providers and fire-providers.

9
~

THE WORST JOURNEY
IN THE WORLD

BY APSLEY CHERRY-GARRARD

Apsley Cherry-Garrard was a member of the Antarctic search party that in November of 1912 discovered the bodies of Robert Falcon Scott and his companions in the remnants of the snow-covered tent where they had perished of exhaustion and starvation. Englishman Scott and his men had failed in their attempt to be the first to reach the South Pole (Norwegian explorer Roald Amundsen had beaten them), then met their doom undertaking the 800-mile trek back to the expedition's permanent base in the McMurdo Sound area.

Even though Scott's journey took place in what was summer in the Antarctic, it involved a terrible ordeal of pushing along on skis while man-hauling their sledges of supplies. Eventually, the survivors of the trek huddled in their tent, unable to go a step farther in the terrible storms that had hounded them since their retreat from the Pole began. Ironically, a depot cache of fuel and food was only a few miles away.

Apsley Cherry-Garrard, a young volunteer for the Scott expedition, which had begun in 1910, was not with the final Scott party. He made a separate Antarctic trek with three men that rivals the Scott experience for hardships endured, but ended without loss of life. Cherry-Garrard's The Worst Journey in the World is an account not only of his own experience, but of Scott's experiences as well. Using Scott's journals, found in the tent with the bodies, Cherry-Garrard describes what happened to Scott and his companions on their terrible retreat from the Pole.

The following excerpt from the book picks up the action on January 19, after Scott, Wilson, Bowers, and Oates had made the overwhelmingly bitter discovery that the Norwegians had beaten them to the Pole. Now, defeated, they have begun their second battle: to return to the safety of the expedition base camp 800 miles away.

No matter whether you're reading about Cherry-Garrard's personal ordeal, or his account of what Scott and his men endured, The Worst Journey in the World *ranks as a classic in survival literature.*

~~~~~~

From Scott's diary:

"The Norwegians have forestalled us and are first at the Pole. It is a terrible disappointment, and I am very sorry for my loyal companions. Many thoughts come and much discussion have we had. Tomorrow we must march on to the Pole and then hasten home with all the speed we can compass. All the day-dreams must go; it will be a wearisome return.

"The Pole. Yes, but under very different circumstances from those expected . . . companions labouring on with cold feet and hands. . . . Evans had such cold hands we camped for lunch . . . the wind is blowing hard, T. -21°, and there is that curious damp, cold feeling in the air which chills one to the bone in no time. . . . Great God! this is an awful place."

Apsley Cherry-Garrard's narration continues as Scott's party faces the dreadful return trip back to their starting base:

All the joy had gone from their sledging. They were hungry, they were cold, the pulling was heavy, and two of them were not fit. As long ago as January 14 Scott wrote that Oates was feeling the cold and fatigue more than the others and again he refers to the matter on January 20. On January 19 Wilson wrote: "We get our hairy faces and mouths dreadfully iced up on the march, and often one's hands very cold indeed holding ski-sticks. Evans, who cut his knuckle some days ago at the last depôt, has a lot of pus in it to-night."

January 20: "Evans has got 4 or 5 of his finger-tips badly blistered by the cold. Titus also his nose and cheeks—al[so] Evans and Bowers."

January 28: "Evans has a number of badly blistered finger-ends which he got at the Pole. Titus' big toe is turning blue-black."

January 31: "Evans' finger-nails all coming off, very raw and sore."

February 4: "Evans is feeling the cold a lot, always getting frost-bitten. Titus' toes are blackening, and his nose and cheeks are dead yellow. Dressing Evans' fingers every other day with boric vaseline: they are quite sweet still . . . Evans' fingers suppurating. Nose very bad [hard] and rotten-looking."

Scott was getting alarmed about Evans, who "has dislodged two finger-nails to-night; his hands are really bad, and, to my surprise, he shows signs of losing heart over it. He hasn't been cheerful since the accident. . . . The party is not improving in condition, especially Evans, who is becoming rather dull and incapable. . . . Evans' nose is almost as bad as his fingers. He is a good deal crocked up."

From Scott's diary, February 17:

"The weather cleared and we got away for a clear run to the depôt and had gone a good part of the way when Evans found his ski shoes coming off. He was allowed to readjust and continue to pull, but it happened again, and then again, so he was told to unhitch, get them right, and follow on and catch us up. He lagged far behind till lunch, and when we camped we had lunch, and then went back for him as he had not come up. He had fallen and had his hands frost-bitten, and we then returned for the sledge, and brought it, and fetched him in on it as he was rapidly losing the use of his legs. He was comatose when we got him into the tent, and he died without recovering consciousness that night, about 10 p.m. We had a short rest for an hour or two in our bags that night, then had a meal and came on through the pressure ridges about 4 miles farther down and reached our Lower Glacier Depôt. Here we camped at last, had a good meal and slept a good night's rest which we badly needed. Our depôt was all right. . . . A very terrible day.

"On discussing the symptoms, we think he began to get weaker just before we reached the Pole, and that his downward path was accelerated first by the shock of his frost-bitten fingers, and later by falls during rough travelling on the glacier, further by his loss of all confidence in himself. Wilson thinks it certain he must have injured his brain by a fall. It is a terrible thing to lose a companion in this way, but calm reflection shows that there could not have been a better ending to the terrible anxieties of the past week. Discussion of the situation at lunch yesterday shows us what a desperate pass we were in with a sick man on our hands at such a distance from home."

Wilson's diary continues:

February 18: "We had only five hours' sleep. We had butter and biscuit and tea when we woke at 2 p.m., then came over the Gap entrance to the pony-slaughter camp, visiting a rock moraine of Mt. Hope on the way."

February 19: "Late in getting away after making up new 10-foot sledge and digging out pony meat. We made 5½ m. on a very heavy surface indeed."

Cherry-Garrard's narration continues:

This bad surface is the feature of their first homeward marches on the Barrier. From now onwards they complain always of the terrible surfaces, but a certain amount of the heavy pulling must be ascribed to their own weakness. In the low temperatures which occurred later, bad surfaces were to be expected: but now the temperatures were not really low, about zero to -17°: fine clear days for the most part and, a thing to be noticed, little wind. They wanted wind, which would probably be behind them from the south.

From Scott's diary:

"Oh! for a little wind. This windless area close to the coast and that, as we are making steadily outwards, we shall shortly escape it. It is perhaps premature [February 19] to be anxious about covering distance. In all other respects things are improving. We have our sleeping-bags spread on the sledge and they are drying, but, above all, we have our full measure of food again. To-night we had a sort of stew fry of pemmican and horseflesh, and voted it the best hoosh we had ever had on a sledge journey. The absence of poor Evans is a help to the commissariat, but if he had been here in a fit state we might have got along faster. I wonder what is in store for us, with some little alarm at the lateness of the season."

And on February 20, when they made 7 miles, Scott writes:

"At present our sledge and ski leave deeply ploughed tracks which can be seen winding for miles behind. It is distressing, but as usual trials are forgotten when we camp, and good food is our lot. Pray God we get better travelling as we are not so fit as we were, and the season is advancing apace."

February 21: "We never won a march of 8½ miles with greater difficulty, but we can't go on like this."

Cherry-Garrard's narration continues:

A breeze suddenly came away from S.S.E., force 4 to 6 at 11 a.m. on February 22, and they hoisted the sail on the sledge they had just picked up. They immediately lost the tracks they were following, and failed to find the cairns and camp remains which they should have picked up if they had been on the right course, which was difficult here owing to the thick weather we had on the outward march. Bowers was sure they were too near the land and they steered out, but still failed to pick up the line on which their depôts and their lives depended. Scott was convinced they were outside, not inside, the line.

The next morning Bowers took a round of angles, and they came to the conclusion, on slender evidence, that they were still too near the land. They had an unhappy march, still off the tracks, "but just as we decided to lunch, Bowers' wonderful sharp eyes detected an old double lunch cairn, the theodolite telescope confirmed it, and our spirits rose accordingly." Then Wilson had another "bad attack of snow-glare: could hardly keep a chink of eye open in goggles to see the course. Fat pony hoosh." This day they reached the Lower Barrier Depôt.

. . . but they would have been all right, these men, if the cold had not come down upon them, a bolt quite literally from the blue of a clear sky: unexpected, unforetold and fatal. The cold itself was not so tremendous until you realize that they had been out four months, that they had fought their way up the biggest glacier in the world in feet of soft snow, that they had spent seven weeks under plateau conditions of rarefied air, big winds and low temperatures, and they had watched one of their companions die—not in a bed, in a hospital or ambulance, nor suddenly, but slowly, night by night and day by day, with his hands frost-bitten and his brain going, until they must have wondered, each man in his heart, whether in such case a human being could be left to die, that four men might live. He died a natural death and they went out on to the Barrier.

Given such conditions as were expected, and the conditions for which preparation had been made, they would have come home alive and well. Some men say the weather was abnormal: there is some evidence that it was. The fact remains that the temperature dropped into the minus thirties by day and the minus forties by night. The fact also remains that there was a great lack of southerly winds, and in consequence the air near the surface was not being mixed: excessive radiation took place, and a layer of cold air formed near the ground. Crystals also formed on the surface of the snow and the wind was not enough to sweep them away. As the temperature dropped, so the surface for the runners of the sledges became worse, as I explained elsewhere. They were pulling as if it were through sand.

In the face of the difficulties which beset them, their marches were magnificent: 11½ miles on February 25 and again on the following day; 12.2 miles on February 27; and 11½ miles again on February 28 and 29. If they could have kept this up they would have come through without a doubt. But I think it was about now that they suspected, and then were sure, that they could not pull through.

Scott's diary, written at lunch, March 2, is as follows:

"Misfortunes rarely come singly. We marched to the [Middle Barrier] depôt fairly easily yesterday afternoon, and since that have suffered three distinct blows which have placed us in a bad position. First, we found a shortage of oil; with most rigid economy it can scarce carry us to the next depôt on this surface [71 miles away]. Second, Titus Oates disclosed his feet, the toes showing very bad indeed, evidently bitten by the late temperatures. The third blow came in the night, when the wind, which we had hailed with some joy, brought dark overcast weather. It fell below -40° in the night, and this morning it took 1½ hours to get our foot-gear on, but we got away before eight. We lost cairn and tracks together and made as steady as we could N. by W., but have seen nothing. Worse was to come—the surface is simply awful. In spite of strong wind and full sail we have only done 5½ miles. We are in a *very* queer street, since there is no doubt we cannot do the extra marches and feel the cold horribly."

They did nearly ten miles that day, but on March 3 they had a terrible time. "God help us," wrote Scott, "we can't keep up this pulling, that is certain. Amongst ourselves we are unendingly cheerful, but what each man feels in his heart I can only guess. Putting on foot-gear in the morning is getting slower and slower, therefore every day more dangerous."

The following extracts are taken from Scott's diary:

Sunday, March 4, Lunch: "We are in a very tight place indeed, but none of us despondent *yet*, or at least we preserve every semblance of good cheer, but one's heart sinks as the sledge stops dead at some sastrugi behind which the surface sand lies thickly heaped. For the moment the temperature is in the -20°—an improvement which makes us much more comfortable, but a colder snap is bound to come again soon. I fear that Oates at least will weather such an event very poorly. Providence to our aid! We can expect little from man now except the possibility of extra food at the next depôt. It will be real bad if we get there and find the same shortage of oil. Shall we get there? Such a short distance it would have appeared to us on the summit! I don't know what I should do if Wilson and Bowers weren't so determinedly cheerful over things."

Monday, March 5, Lunch: "Regret to say going from bad to worse. We got a slant of wind yesterday afternoon, and going on 5 hours we converted our wretched morning run of 3½ miles into something over 9. We went to bed on a cup of cocoa and pemmican solid with the chill off. . . . The result is telling on all, but mainly on Oates, whose feet are in a wretched condition. One swelled up tremendously last night and he is very lame this morning. We started march on tea and pemmican as last night—we pretend to prefer the pemmican this way. Marched for 5 hours this morning over a slightly better surface covered with high moundy sastrugi. Sledge capsized twice; we pulled on foot, covering about 5½ miles. We are two pony marches and 4 miles about from our depôt. Our fuel dreadfully low and the poor Soldier nearly done. It is pathetic enough because we can do nothing for him; more hot food might do a little, but only a little, I fear. We none of us expected these terribly low temperatures, and of the rest of us, Wilson is feeling them most; mainly, I fear, from his self-sacrificing devotion in doctoring Oates' feet. We cannot help each other; each has enough to do to take care of himself. We get cold on the march when the trudging is heavy, and the wind pierces our worn garments. The others, all of them, are unendingly cheerful when in the tent. We mean to see the game through with a proper spirit, but it's tough work to be pulling harder than we ever pulled in our lives for long hours, and to feel that the progress is so slow. One can only say 'God help us!' and plod on our weary way, cold and very miserable, though outwardly cheerful. We talk of all sorts of subjects in the tent, not much of food now, since we decided to take the risk of running a full ration. We simply couldn't go hungry at this time."

Tuesday, March 6, Lunch: "We did a little better with help of wind yesterday afternoon, finishing 9½ miles for the day, and 27 miles from depôt. But this morning things have been awful. It was warm in the night, and for the first time during the journey I overslept myself by more than an hour; then we were slow with foot-gear; then, pulling with all our might (for our lives) we could scarcely advance at rate of a mile an hour; then it grew thick and three times we had to get out of harness to search for tracks. The result is something less than 3½ miles for the forenoon. The sun is shining now and the wind gone. Poor Oates is unable to pull, sits on the sledge when we are track-searching—he is wonderfully plucky, as his feet must be giving him great pain. He makes no complaint, but his spirits only come up in spurts now, and he grows more silent in the tent. We are making a spirit lamp to try and replace the primus when our oil is exhausted."

Wednesday, March 7, Lunch: "A little worse, I fear. One of Oates' feet *very* bad this morning; he is wonderfully brave. We still talk of what we will do together at home.

"We only made 6½ miles yesterday. This morning in 4½ hours we did just over 4 miles. We are 16 from our depôt. If we only find the correct proportion of food there and this surface continues, we may get to the next depôt [Mt. Hooper, 72 miles farther], but not to One Ton Camp. We hope against hope that the dogs have been to Mt. Hooper; then we might pull through. If there is a shortage of oil again, we can have little hope. One feels that for poor Oates the crisis is near, but none of us are improving, though we are wonderfully fit considering the really excessive work we are doing. We are only kept going by good food. No wind this morning till a chill northerly air came ahead. Sun bright and cairns showing up well. I should like to keep the track to the end."

Thursday, March 8, Lunch: "Worse and worse in morning; poor Oates' left foot can never last out, and time over foot-gear something awful. Have to wait in night foot-gear for nearly an hour before I start changing, and then am generally first to be ready. Wilson's feet giving trouble now, but this mainly because he gives so much help to others. We did 4½ miles this morning and are now 8½ miles from the depôt—a ridiculously small distance to feel in difficulties, yet on this surface we know we cannot equal half our old marches, and that for that effort we expend nearly double the energy. The great question is: What shall we find at the depôt? If the dogs have visited it we may get along a good distance, but if there is another short allowance of fuel, God help us indeed. We are in a very bad way, I fear, in any case."

Saturday, March 10: "Things steadily downhill. Oates' foot worse. He has rare pluck and must know that he can never get through. He asked Wilson if he had a chance this morning, and of course Bill had to say he didn't know. In point of fact he has none. Apart from him, if he went under now, I doubt whether we could get through. With great care we might have a dog's chance, but no more. The weather conditions are awful, and our gear gets steadily more icy and difficult to manage. . . .

"Yesterday we marched up the depôt, Mt. Hooper. Cold comfort. Shortage on our allowance all round. I don't know that any one is to blame. The dogs which would have been our salvation have evidently failed. Meares had a bad trip home I suppose.

"This morning it was calm when we breakfasted, but the wind came from the W.N.W. as we broke camp. It rapidly grew in strength. After travelling for half an hour I saw that none of us could go on facing such conditions. We were forced to camp and are spending the rest of the day in a comfortless blizzard camp, wind quite foul."

Sunday, March 11: "Titus Oates is very near the end, one feels. What we or he will do, God only knows. We discussed the matter after breakfast; he is a brave fine fellow and understands the situation, but he practically asked for advice. Nothing could be said but to urge him to march as long as he could. One satisfactory result to the discussion: I practically ordered Wilson to hand over the means of ending our troubles to us, so that any one of us may know how to do so. Wilson had no choice between doing so and our ransacking the medicine case. We have 30 opium tabloids apiece and he is left with a tube of morphine. So far the tragical side of our story.

"The sky completely overcast when we started this morning. We could see nothing, lost the tracks, and doubtless have been swaying a good deal since—3.1 miles for the forenoon—terribly heavy dragging—expected it. Know that 6 miles is about the limit of our endurance now, if we get no help from wind or surfaces. We have 7 days' food and should be about 55 miles from One Ton Camp to-night, $6 \times 7 = 42$, leaving us 13 miles short of our distance, even if things get no worse. Meanwhile the season rapidly advances."

Monday, March 12: "We did 6.9 miles yesterday, under our necessary average. Things are left much the same, Oates not pulling much, and now with hands as well as feet pretty well useless. We did 4 miles this morning in 4 hours 20 min.—we may hope for 3 this afternoon, $7 \times 6 = 42$. We shall be 47 miles from the depôt. I doubt if we can possibly do it. The surface remains awful, the cold intense, and our physical condition running down. God help us! Not a breath of favourable wind for more than a week, and apparently liable to head winds at any moment."

Wednesday, March 14: "No doubt about the going downhill, but everything going wrong for us. Yesterday we woke to a strong northerly wind with temp. -37°. Couldn't face it, so remained in camp till 2, then did 5¼ miles. Wanted to march later, but party feeling the cold badly as the breeze (N.) never took off entirely, and as the sun sank, the temp. fell. Long time getting supper in dark.

"This morning started with southerly breeze, set sail and passed another cairn at good speed; half-way, however, the wind shifted to W. by S. or W.S.W., blew through our wind-clothes and into our mitts. Poor Wilson horribly cold, could [not] get off ski for some time. Bowers and I practically made camp, and when we got into the tent at last we were all deadly cold. Then temp. now mid-day down -43° and the wind strong. We *must* go on, but now the making of every camp must be more difficult and dangerous. It must be near the end, but a pretty merciful end. Poor Oates got it again in the foot. I shudder to think what it will be like to-morrow. It is only with greatest pains rest of us keep off frost-bites. No idea there could be temperatures like this at this time of year with such winds. Truly awful outside the tent. Must fight it out to the last biscuit, but can't reduce rations."

Friday, March 16, or Saturday, March 17: "Lost track of dates, but think the last correct. Tragedy all along the line. At lunch, the day before yesterday, poor Titus Oates said he couldn't go on; he proposed we should leave him in his sleeping-bag. That we could not do, and we induced him to come on, on the afternoon march. In spite of its awful nature for him he struggled on and we made a few miles. At night he was worse and we knew the end had come.

"Should this be found I want these facts recorded. Oates' last thoughts were of his mother, but immediately before he took pride in thinking that his regiment would be pleased with the bold way in which he met his death. We can testify to his bravery. He has borne intense suffering for weeks without complaint, and to the very last was able and willing to discuss outside subjects. He did not—would not—give up hope till the very end. He was a brave soul. This was the end. He slept through the night before last, hoping not to wake; but he woke in the morning—yesterday. It was blowing a blizzard. He said, 'I am just going outside and may be some time.' He went out into the blizzard and we have not seen him since.

"I take this opportunity of saying that we have stuck to our sick companions to the last. In [the] case of Edgar Evans, when absolutely out of food and he lay insensible, the safety of the remainder seemed to demand his abandonment, but Providence mercifully removed him at this critical moment. He died a natural death, and we did not leave him till two hours after his death. We knew that poor Oates was walking to his death, but though we tried to dissuade him, we knew it was the act of a brave man and an English gentleman. We all hope to meet the end with a similar spirit, and assuredly the end is not far.

"I can only write at lunch and then only occasionally. The cold is intense, -40° at mid-day. My companions are unendingly cheerful, but we are all on the verge of serious frost-bites, and though we constantly talk of fetching through I don't think any one of us believes it in his heart.

"We are cold on the march now, and at all times except meals. Yesterday we had to lay up for a blizzard and to-day we move dreadfully slowly. We are at No. 14 Pony Camp, only two pony marches from One Ton Depôt. We leave here our theodolite, a camera, and Oates' sleeping-bags. Diaries, etc., and geological specimens carried at Wilson's special request, will be found with us or on our sledge."

Sunday, March 18: "To-day, lunch, we are 21 miles from the depôt. Ill fortune presses, but better may come. We have had more wind and drift from ahead yesterday; had to stop marching; wind N.W., force 4, temp. -35°. No human being could face it, and we are worn out *nearly*.

"My right foot has gone, nearly all the toes—two days ago I was proud possessor of best feet. . . . Bowers takes first place in condition, but there is not much to choose after all. The others are still confident of getting through—or pretend to be—I don't know! We have the last *half* fill of oil in our primus and a very small quantity of spirit—this alone between us and thirst. The wind is fair for the moment, and that is perhaps a fact to help. The mileage would have seemed ridiculously small on our outward journey."

Monday, March 19, Lunch: "We camped with difficulty last night and were dreadfully cold till after our supper of cold pemmican and biscuit and a half pannikin of cocoa cooked over the spirit. Then, contrary to expectation, we got warm and all slept well. To-day we started in the usual dragging manner. Sledge dreadfully heavy. We are 15½ miles from the depôt and ought to get there in three days. What progress! We have two days' food but barely a day's fuel. All our feet are getting bad—Wilson's best, my right foot worse, left all right. There is no chance to nurse one's feet till we can get hot food into us. Amputation is the least I can hope for now, but will the trouble spread? That is the serious question. The weather doesn't give us a chance—the wind from N. to N.W. and -40° temp, to-day."

Wednesday, March 21: "Got within 11 miles of depôt Monday night; had to lay up all yesterday in severe blizzard. To-day forlorn hope, Wilson and Bowers going to depôt for fuel."

Thursday, March 22 and Friday, March 23: "Blizzard bad as ever—Wilson and Bowers unable to start—to-morrow last chance—no fuel and only one or two [days' worth] of food left—must be near the end. Have decided it shall be natural—we shall march for the depôt with or without our effects and die in our tracks."

Thursday, March 29: "Since the 21st we have had a continuous gale from W.S.W. and S.W. We had fuel to make two cups of tea apiece and bare food for two days on the 20th. Every day we have been ready to start for our depot *11 miles* away, but outside the door of the tent it remains a scene of whirling drift. I do not think we can hope for any better things now. We shall stick it out to the end, but we are getting weaker, of course, and the end cannot be far.

"It seems a pity, but I do not think I can write more.

—R. Scott."

Last entry: "For God's sake, look after our people."

Apsley Cherry-Garrard on the discovery of Scott's final tent, November 1912:

Nearly mid-day. 11–12 miles south of One Ton. We have found them—to say it has been a ghastly day cannot express it—it is too bad for words. The tent was there, about half-a-mile to the west of our course, and close to a drifted-up cairn of last year. It was covered with snow and looked just like a cairn, only an extra gathering of snow showing where the ventilator was, and so we found the door.

It was drifted up some 2–3 feet to windward. Just by the side two pairs of ski sticks, or the topmost half of them, appeared over the snow, and a bamboo which proved to be the mast of the sledge.

Their story I am not going to try and put down. They got to this point on March 21, and on the 29th all was over.

Nor will I try and put down what there was in that tent. Scott lay in the centre, Bill on his left, with his head towards the door, and Birdie [Bowers] on his right, lying with his feet towards the door.

Bill especially had died very quietly with his hands folded over his chest. Birdie also quietly.

Oates' death was a very fine one. We go on to-morrow to try and find his body. He was glad that his regiment would be proud of him.

They reached the Pole a month after Amundsen.

We have everything—records, diaries, etc. They have among other things several rolls of photographs, a meteorological log kept up to March 13, and, considering all things, a great many geological specimens. *And they have stuck to everything.* It is magnificent that men in such case should go on pulling everything that they have died to gain. I think they realized their coming end a long time before. By Scott's head was tobacco: there is also a bag of tea.

Atkinson gathered every one together and read to them the account of Oates' death given in Scott's diary: Scott expressly states that he wished it known. His (Scott's) last words are:

"For God's sake, take care of our people."

Then Atkinson read the lesson from the Burial Service from Corinthians. Perhaps it has never been read in a more magnificent cathedral and under more impressive circumstances—for it is a grave which kings must envy. Then some prayers from the Burial Service: and there with the floor-cloth under them and the tent above we buried them in their sleeping-bags—and surely their work has not been in vain.

That scene can never leave my memory. We with the dogs had seen Wright turn away from the course by himself and the mule party swerve right-handed ahead of us. He had seen what he thought was a cairn, and then something looking black by its side. A vague kind of wonder gradually gave way to a real alarm. We came up to them all halted. Wright came across to us. "It is the tent," [he said]. I do not know how he knew. Just a waste of snow: to our right the remains of one of last year's cairns, a mere mound: and then three feet of bamboo sticking quite alone out of the snow: and then another mound, of snow, perhaps a trifle more pointed. We walked up to it. I do not think we quite realized—not for very long—but some one reached up to a projection of snow, and brushed it away. The green flap of the ventilator of the tent appeared, and we knew that the door was below.

Two of us entered, through the funnel of the outer tent, and through the bamboos on which was stretched the lining of the inner tent. There was some snow—not much—between the two linings. But inside we could see nothing—the snow had drifted out the light. There was nothing to do but to dig the tent out. Soon we could see the outlines. There were three men here.

Bowers and Wilson were sleeping in their bags. Scott had thrown back the flaps of his bag at the end. His left hand was stretched over

Wilson, his lifelong friend. Beneath the head of his bag, between the bag and the floor-cloth, was the green wallet in which he carried his diary. The brown books of diary were inside: and on the floor-cloth were some letters.

Everything was tidy. The tent had been pitched as well as ever, with the door facing down the sastrugi, the bamboos with a good spread, the tent itself taut and shipshape. There was no snow inside the inner lining. There were some loose pannikins from the cooker, the ordinary tent gear, the personal belongings and a few more letters and records—personal and scientific. Near Scott was a lamp formed from a tin and some lamp wick off a finnesko. It had been used to burn the little methylated spirit which remained. I think that Scott had used it to help him to write up to the end. I feel sure that he had died last—and once I had thought that he would not go so far as some of the others. We never realized how strong that man was, mentally and physically, until now.

We sorted out the gear, records, papers, diaries, spare clothing, letters, chronometers, finnesko, socks, a flag. There was even a book which I had lent Bill for the journey—and he had brought it back. Somehow we learnt that Amundsen had been to the Pole, and that they too had been to the Pole, and both items of news seemed to be of no importance whatever. There was a letter there from Amundsen to King Haakon. There were the personal chatty little notes we had left for them on the Beardmore—how much more important to us than all the royal letters in the world.

We dug down the bamboo which had brought us to this place. It led to the sledge, many feet down, and had been rigged there as a mast. And on the sledge were some more odds and ends—a piece of paper from the biscuit box: Bowers' meteorological log: and the geological specimens, thirty pounds of them, all of the first importance. Drifted over also were the harnesses, ski and ski-sticks.

Hour after hour, so it seemed to me, Atkinson sat in our tent and read. The finder was to read the diary and then it was to be brought home—these were Scott's instructions written on the cover. But Atkinson said he was only going to read sufficient to know what had happened—and after that they were brought home unopened and unread. When he had the outline we all gathered together and he read to us the Message to the Public, and the account of Oates' death, which Scott had expressly wished to be known.

We never moved them. We took the bamboos of the tent away, and the tent itself covered them. And over them we built the cairn.

I do not know how long we were there, but when all was finished, and the chapter of Corinthians had been read, it was midnight of some day. The sun was dipping low above the Pole, the Barrier was almost in shadow. And the sky was blazing—sheets and sheets of iridescent clouds. The cairn and Cross stood dark against a glory of burnished gold.

Editor's Note: Among the notes and letters Scott had written, discovered in the final tent, was the following profound text:

MESSAGE TO THE PUBLIC

The causes of the disaster are not due to faulty organization, but to misfortune in all risks which had to be undertaken:

1. The loss of pony transport in March 1911 obliged me to start later than I had intended, and obliged the limits of stuff transported to be narrowed.
2. The weather throughout the outward journey, and especially the long gale in 83° S., stopped us.
3. The soft snow in lower reaches of glacier again reduced pace.

We fought these untoward events with a will and conquered, but it cut into our provision reserve.

Every detail of our food supplies, clothing and depôts made on the interior ice-sheet and over that long stretch of 700 miles to the Pole and back, worked out to perfection. The advance party would have returned to the glacier in fine form and with surplus of food, but for the astonishing failure of the man whom we had least expected to fail. Edgar Evans was thought the strongest man of the party.

The Beardmore Glacier is not difficult in fine weather, but on our return we did not get a single completely fine day; this with a sick companion enormously increased our anxieties.

As I have said elsewhere, we got into frightfully rough ice and Edgar Evans received a concussion of the brain—he died a natural death, but left us a shaken party with the season unduly advanced.

But all the facts above enumerated were as nothing to the surprise which awaited us on the Barrier. I maintain that our arrangements for returning were quite adequate, and that no one in the world would have expected the temperatures and surfaces which we encountered at this time of the year. On the summit in lat. 85°–86° we had -20°, -30°. On the Barrier in lat. 82°, 10,000 feet lower, we had -30° in the day, -47° at night pretty regularly, with continuous head-wind during our day marches. It is clear that these circumstances come on very suddenly, and our wreck is certainly due to this sudden advent of severe weather, which does not seem to have any satisfactory cause. I do not think human beings ever came through such a month as we have come through, and we should have got through in spite of the weather but for the sickening of a second companion, Captain Oates, and a shortage of fuel in our depôts for which I cannot account, and finally, but for the storm which has fallen on us within 11 miles of the depôt at which we hoped to secure our final supplies.

Surely misfortune could scarcely have exceeded this last blow. We arrived within 11 miles of our old One Ton Camp with fuel for one last meal and food for two days. For four days we have been unable to leave the tent—the gale howling about us. We are weak, writing is difficult, but for my own sake I do not regret this journey, which has shown that Englishmen can endure hardships, help one another, and meet death with as great a fortitude as ever in the past. We took risks, we knew we took them; things have come out against us, and therefore we have no cause for complaint, but bow to the will of Providence, determined still to do our best to the last. But if we have been willing to give our lives to this enterprise, which is for the honour of our country, I appeal to our countrymen to see that those who depend on us are properly cared for.

Had we lived, I should have had a tale to tell of the hardihood, endurance, and courage of my companions which would have stirred the heart of every Englishman. These rough notes and our dead bodies must tell the tale, but surely, surely a great rich country like ours will see that those who are dependent on us are properly provided for.

—R. SCOTT.

10

LOVE OF LIFE

BY JACK LONDON

When you're alone in the Klondike wilds—without food, guns, and gear, even proper clothing—escape is a teasing thought. You might as well lie down and die. Right? Master storyteller of Northern adventures, Jack London, shows the strength behind these famous words: Never give up! Never, ever give up!

They limped painfully down the bank, and once the foremost of the two men staggered among the rough-strewn rocks. They were tired and weak, and their faces had the drawn expression of patience which comes of hardship long endured. They were heavily burdened with blanket packs which were strapped to their shoulders. Head-straps, passing across the forehead, helped support these packs. Each man carried a rifle. They walked in a stooped posture, the shoulders well forward, the head still farther forward, the eyes bent upon the ground.

"I wish we had just about two of them cartridges that's layin' in that cache of ourn," said the second man.

His voice was utterly and drearily expressionless. He spoke without enthusiasm; and the first man, limping into the milky stream that foamed over the rocks, vouchsafed no reply.

The other man followed at his heels. They did not remove their footgear, though the water was icy cold—so cold that their ankles ached and their feet went numb. In places the water dashed against their knees, and both men staggered for footing.

The man who followed slipped on a smooth boulder, nearly fell, but recovered himself with a violent effort, at the same time uttering a sharp exclamation of pain. He seemed faint and dizzy and put out his free hand while he reeled, as though seeking support against the air. When he had steadied himself he stepped forward, but reeled again and nearly fell. Then he stood still and looked at the other man, who had never turned his head.

The man stood still for fully a minute, as though debating with himself. Then he called out:

"I say, Bill, I've sprained my ankle."

Bill staggered on through the milky water. He did not look around. The man watched him go, and though his face was expressionless as ever, his eyes were like the eyes of a wounded deer.

The other man limped up the farther bank and continued straight on without looking back. The man in the stream watched him. His lips trembled a little, so that the rough thatch of brown hair which covered them was visibly agitated. His tongue even strayed out to moisten them.

"Bill!" he cried out.

It was the pleading cry of a strong man in distress, but Bill's head did not turn. The man watched him go, limping grotesquely and lurching forward with stammering gait up the slow slope toward the soft sky-line of the low-lying hill. He watched him go till he passed over the crest and disappeared. Then he turned his gaze and slowly took in the circle of the world that remained to him now that Bill was gone.

Near the horizon the sun was smouldering dimly, almost obscured by formless mists and vapors, which gave an impression of mass and density without outline or tangibility. The man pulled out his watch, the while resting his weight on one leg. It was four o'clock, and as the season was near the last of July or first of August—he did not know the precise date within a week or two—he knew that the sun roughly marked the northwest. He looked to the south and knew that some-where beyond those bleak hills lay the Great Bear Lake; also, he knew that in that direction the Arctic Circle cut its forbidding way across the Canadian Barrens. This stream in which he stood was a feeder to the Coppermine River, which in turn flowed north and emptied into Coronation Gulf and the Arctic Ocean. He had never been there, but he had seen it, once, on a Hudson Bay Company chart.

Again his gaze completed the circle of the world about him. It was not a heartening spectacle. Everywhere was soft sky-line. The hills were all low-lying. There were no trees, no shrubs, no grasses—naught but a tremendous and terrible desolation that sent fear swiftly dawning into his eyes.

"Bill!" he whispered, once and twice. "Bill!"

He cowered in the midst of the milky water, as though the vastness were pressing in upon him with overwhelming force, brutally crushing him with its complacent awfulness. He began to shake as with an ague-fit, till the gun fell from his hand with a splash. This served to rouse him. He fought with his fear and pulled himself together, groping in the water and recovering the weapon. He hitched his pack farther over on his left shoulder, so as to take a portion of its weight from off the injured ankle. Then he proceeded, slowly and carefully, wincing with pain, to the bank.

He did not stop. With a desperation that was madness, unmindful of the pain, he hurried up the slope to the crest of the hill over which his comrade had disappeared—more grotesque and comical by far than that limping, jerking comrade. But at the crest he saw a shallow valley, empty of life. He fought with his fear again, overcame it, hitched the pack still farther over on his left shoulder, and lurched on down the slope.

The bottom of the valley was soggy with water, which the thick moss held, spongelike, close to the surface. This water squirted out from under his feet at every step, and each time he lifted a foot the action culminated in a sucking sound as the wet moss reluctantly released its grip. He picked his way from muskeg to muskeg, and followed the other man's footsteps along and across the rocky ledges which thrust like islets through the sea of moss.

Though alone, he was not lost. Farther on he knew he would come to where dead spruce and fir, very small and weazened, bordered the shore of a little lake, the titchin-nichilie, in the tongue of the country, the "land of little sticks." And into that lake flowed a small stream, the water of which was not milky. There was rush-grass on that stream—this he remembered well—but no timber, and he would follow it till its first trickle ceased at a divide. He would cross this divide to the first trickle of another stream, flowing to the west, which he would follow until it emptied into the river Dease, and here he would find a cache under an upturned canoe and piled over with many rocks. And in this cache would be ammunition for his empty gun, fish-hooks and lines, a small net—all the utilities for the killing and snaring of food. Also, he would find flour—not much—a piece of bacon, and some beans.

Bill would be waiting for him there, and they would paddle away south down the Dease to the Great Bear Lake. And south across the lake they would go, ever south, till they gained the Mackenzie. And south, still south, they would go, while the winter raced vainly after them, and the ice formed in the eddies, and the days grew chilly and crisp, south to some warm Hudson Bay Company post, where timber grew tall and generous and there was grub without end.

These were the thoughts of the man as he strove onward. But hard as he strove with his body, he strove equally hard with his mind, trying to think that Bill had not deserted him, that Bill would surely wait for him at the cache. He was compelled to think this thought, or else there would not be any use to strive, and he would have lain down and died. And as the dim ball of the sun sank slowly into the northwest he covered every inch—and many times—of his and Bill's flight south before the down coming winter. And he conned the grub of the cache and the grub of the Hudson Bay Company post over and over again. He had not eaten for two days; for a far longer time he had not had all he wanted to eat. Often he stooped and picked pale muskeg berries, put them into his mouth, and chewed and swallowed them. A muskeg berry is a bit of seed enclosed in a bit of water. In the mouth the water melts away and the seed chews sharp and bitter. The man knew there was no nourishment in the berries, but he chewed them patiently with a hope greater than knowledge and defying experience.

At nine o'clock he stubbed his toe on a rocky ledge, and from sheer weariness and weakness staggered and fell. He lay for some time, without movement, on his side. Then he slipped out of the pack-straps and clumsily dragged himself into a sitting posture. It was not yet dark, and in the lingering twilight he groped about among the rocks for shreds of dry moss. When he had gathered a heap he built a fire—a smouldering, smudgy fire—and put a tin pot of water on to boil.

He unwrapped his pack and the first thing he did was to count his matches. There were sixty-seven. He counted them three times to make sure. He divided them into several portions, wrapping them in oil paper, disposing of one bunch in his empty tobacco pouch, of another bunch in the inside band of his battered hat, of a third bunch under his shirt on the chest. This accomplished, a panic came upon him, and he unwrapped them all and counted them again. There were still sixty-seven.

He dried his wet foot-gear by the fire. The moccasins were in soggy shreds. The blanket socks were worn through in places, and his feet were raw and bleeding. His ankle was throbbing, and he gave it an examination. It had swollen to the size of his knee. He tore a long strip from one of his two blankets and bound the ankle tightly. He tore other strips and bound them about his feet to serve for both moccasins and socks. Then he drank the pot of water, steaming hot, wound his watch, and crawled between his blankets.

He slept like a dead man. The brief darkness around midnight came and went. The sun arose in the northeast—at least the day dawned in that quarter, for the sun was hidden by gray clouds.

At six o'clock he awoke, quietly lying on his back. He gazed straight up into the gray sky and knew that he was hungry. As he rolled over on his elbow he was startled by a loud snort, and saw a bull caribou regarding him with alert curiosity. The animal was not more than fifty feet away, and instantly into the man's mind leaped the vision and the savor of a caribou steak sizzling and frying over a fire. Mechanically he reached for the empty gun, drew a bead, and pulled the trigger. The bull snorted and leaped away, his hoofs rattling and clattering as he fled across the ledges.

The man cursed and flung the empty gun from him. He groaned aloud as he started to drag himself to his feet. It was a slow and arduous task. His joints were like rusty hinges. They worked harshly in their sockets, with much friction, and each bending or unbending was accomplished only through a sheer exertion of will. When he finally gained his feet, another minute or so was consumed in straightening up, so that he could stand erect as a man should stand.

He crawled up a small knoll and surveyed the prospect. There were no trees, no bushes, nothing but a gray sea of moss scarcely diversified by gray rocks, gray lakelets, and gray streamlets. The sky was gray. There was no sun nor hint of sun. He had no idea of north, and he had forgotten the way he had come to this spot the night before. But he was not lost. He knew that. Soon he would come to the land of the little sticks. He felt that it lay off to the left somewhere, not far—possibly just over the next low hill.

He went back to put his pack into shape for traveling. He assured himself of the existence of his three separate parcels of matches, though he did not stop to count them. But he did linger, debating, over a squat moose-hide sack. It was not large. He could hide it under his two hands. He knew that it weighed fifteen pounds—as much as all the rest of the pack—and it worried him. He finally set it to one side and proceeded to roll the pack. He paused to gaze at the squat moose-hide sack. He picked it up hastily with a defiant glance about him, as though the desolation were trying to rob him of it; and when he rose to his feet to stagger on into the day, it was included in the pack on his back.

He bore away to the left, stopping now and again to eat muskeg berries. His ankle had stiffened, his limp was more pronounced, but the pain of it was as nothing compared with the pain of his stomach. The hunger pangs were sharp. They gnawed and gnawed until he could not keep his mind steady on the course he must pursue to gain the land of little sticks. The muskeg berries did not allay this gnawing, while they made his tongue and the roof of his mouth sore with their irritating bite.

He came upon a valley where rock ptarmigan rose on whirring wings from the ledges and muskegs. *Ker—ker—ker* was the cry they made. He threw stones at them, but could not hit them. He placed his pack on the ground and stalked them as a cat stalks a sparrow. The sharp rocks cut through his pants' legs till his knees left a trail of blood; but the hurt was lost in the hurt of his hunger. He squirmed over the wet moss, saturating his clothes and chilling his body; but he was not aware of it, so great was his fever for food. And always the ptarmigan rose, whirring, before him, till their *ker—ker—ker* became a mock to him, and he cursed them and cried aloud at them with their own cry.

Once he crawled upon one that must have been asleep. He did not see it till it shot up in his face from its rocky nook. He made a clutch as startled as was the rise of the ptarmigan, and there remained in his hand three tail-feathers. As he watched its flight he hated it, as though it had done him some terrible wrong. Then he returned and shouldered his pack.

As the day wore along he came into valleys or swales where game was more plentiful. A band of caribou passed by, twenty and odd animals, tantalizingly within rifle range. He felt a wild desire to run after them, a certitude that he could run them down. A black fox came toward him, carrying a ptarmigan in his mouth. The man shouted. It was a fearful cry, but the fox, leaping away in fright, did not drop the ptarmigan.

Late in the afternoon he followed a stream, milky with lime, which ran through sparse patches of rush-grass. Grasping these rushes firmly near the root, he pulled up what resembled a young onion-sprout no larger than a shingle-nail. It was tender, and his teeth sank into it with a crunch that promised deliciously of food. But its fibers were tough. It was composed of stringy filaments saturated with water, like the berries, and devoid of nourishment. He threw off his pack and went into the rush-grass on hands and knees, crunching and munching, like some bovine creature.

He was very weary and often wished to rest—to lie down and sleep; but he was continually driven on—not so much by his desire to gain the land of little sticks as by his hunger. He searched little ponds for frogs and dug up the earth with his nails for worms, though he knew in spite that neither frogs nor worms existed so far north.

He looked into every pool of water vainly, until, as the long twilight came on, he discovered a solitary fish, the size of a minnow, in such a pool. He plunged his arm in up to the shoulder, but it eluded him.

He reached for it with both hands and stirred up the milky mud at the bottom. In his excitement he fell in, wetting himself to the waist. Then the water was too muddy to admit of his seeing the fish, and he was compelled to wait until the sediment had settled.

The pursuit was renewed, till the water was again muddied. But he could not wait. He unstrapped the tin bucket and began to bale the pool. He baled wildly at first, splashing himself and flinging the water so short a distance that it ran back into the pool. He worked more carefully, striving to be cool, though his heart was pounding against his chest and his hands were trembling. At the end of half an hour the pool was nearly dry. Not a cupful of water remained. And there was no fish. He found a hidden crevice among the stones through which it had escaped to the adjoining and larger pool—a pool which he could not empty in a night and a day. Had he known of the crevice, he could have closed it with a rock at the beginning and the fish would have been his.

Thus he thought, and crumpled up and sank down upon the wet earth. At first he cried softly to himself, then he cried loudly to the pitiless desolation that ringed him around; and for a long time after he was shaken by great dry sobs.

He built a fire and warmed himself by drinking quarts of hot water, and made camp on a rocky ledge in the same fashion he had the night before. The last thing he did was to see that his matches were dry and to wind his watch. The blankets were wet and clammy. His ankle pulsed with pain. But he knew only that he was hungry, and through his restless sleep he dreamed of feasts and banquets and of food served and spread in all imaginable ways.

He awoke chilled and sick. There was no sun. The gray of earth and sky had become deeper, more profound. A raw wind was blowing, and the first flurries of snow were whitening the hilltops. The air about him thickened and grew white while he made a fire and boiled more water. It was wet snow, half rain, and the flakes were large and soggy. At first they melted as soon as they came in contact with the earth, but ever more fell, covering the ground, putting out the fire, spoiling his supply of moss-fuel.

This was a signal for him to strap on his pack and stumble onward, he knew not where. He was not concerned with the land of little sticks, nor with Bill and the cache under the upturned canoe by the river Dease. He was mastered by the verb "to eat." He was hunger-mad. He took no heed of the course he pursued, so long as that course led him through the swale bottoms. He felt his way through the wet snow to the watery muskeg berries, and went by feel as he pulled up the rush-grass by the roots. But it was tasteless stuff and did not satisfy. He found a weed that tasted sour and he ate all he could find of it, which was not much, for it was a creeping growth, easily hidden under the several inches of snow.

He had no fire that night, nor hot water, and crawled under his blanket to sleep the broken hunger-sleep. The snow turned into a cold rain. He awakened many times to feel it falling on his upturned face. Day came—a gray day and no sun. It had ceased raining. The keenness of his hunger had departed. Sensibility, as far as concerned the yearning for food, had been exhausted. There was a dull, heavy ache in his stomach, but it did not bother him so much. He was more rational, and once more he was chiefly interested in the land of little sticks and the cache by the river Dease.

He ripped the remnant of one of his blankets into strips and bound his bleeding feet. Also, he recinched the injured ankle and prepared himself for a day of travel. When he came to his pack, he paused long over the squat moose-hide sack, but in the end it went with him.

The snow had melted under the rain, and only the hilltops showed white. The sun came out, and he succeeded in locating the points of the compass, though he knew now that he was lost. Perhaps, in his previous days' wanderings, he had edged away too far to the left. He now bore off to the right to counteract the possible deviation from his true course.

Though the hunger pangs were no longer so exquisite, he realized that he was weak. He was compelled to pause for frequent rests, when he attacked the muskeg berries and rush-grass patches. His tongue felt dry and large, as though covered with a fine hairy growth, and it tasted bitter in his mouth. His heart gave him a great deal of trouble. When he had travelled a few minutes it would begin a remorseless thump, thump, thump, and then leap up and away in a painful flutter of beats that choked him and made him go faint and dizzy.

In the middle of the day he found two minnows in a large pool. It was impossible to bale it, but he was calmer now and managed to catch them in his tin bucket. They were no longer than his little finger, but he was not particularly hungry. The dull ache in his stomach had been growing duller and fainter. It seemed almost that his stomach was dozing. He ate the fish raw, masticating with painstaking care, for the eating was an act of pure reason. While he had no desire to eat, he knew that he must eat to live.

In the evening he caught three more minnows, eating two and saving the third for breakfast. The sun had dried stray shreds of moss, and he was able to warm himself with hot water. He had not covered more than ten miles that day; and the next day, travelling whenever his heart permitted him, he covered no more than five miles. But his stomach did not give him the slightest uneasiness. It had gone to sleep. He was in a strange country, too, and the caribou were growing more plentiful, also the wolves. Often their yelps drifted across the desolation, and once he saw three of them slinking away before his path.

Another night; and in the morning, being more rational, he untied the leather string that fastened the squat moose-hide sack. From its open mouth poured a yellow stream of coarse gold-dust and nuggets. He roughly divided the gold in halves, caching one half on a prominent ledge, wrapped in a piece of blanket, and returning the other half to the sack. He also began to use strips of the one remaining blanket for his feet. He still clung to his gun, for there were cartridges in that cache by the river Dease.

This was a day of fog, and this day hunger awoke in him again. He was very weak and was afflicted with a giddiness which at times blinded him. It was no uncommon thing now for him to stumble and fall; and stumbling once, he fell squarely into a ptarmigan nest. There were four newly hatched chicks, a day old—little specks of pulsating life no more than a mouthful; and he ate them ravenously, thrusting them alive into his mouth and crunching them like eggshells between his teeth. The mother ptarmigan beat about him with great outcry. He used his gun as a club with which to knock her over, but she dodged out of reach. He threw stones at her and with one chance shot broke a wing. Then she fluttered away, running, trailing the broken wing, with him in pursuit.

The little chicks had no more than whetted his appetite. He hopped and bobbed clumsily along on his injured ankle, throwing stones and screaming hoarsely at times; at other times hopping and bobbing silently along, picking himself up grimly and patiently when he fell, or rubbing his eyes with his hand when the giddiness threatened to overpower him.

The chase led him across swampy ground in the bottom of the valley, and he came upon footprints in the soggy moss. They were not his own—he could see that. They must be Bill's. But he could not stop, for the mother ptarmigan was running on. He would catch her first, then he would return and investigate.

He exhausted the mother ptarmigan; but he exhausted himself. She lay panting on her side. He lay panting on his side, a dozen feet away, unable to crawl to her. And as he recovered she recovered, fluttering out of reach as his hungry hand went out to her. The chase was resumed. Night settled down and she escaped. He stumbled from weakness and pitched head foremost on his face, cutting his cheek, his pack upon his back. He did not move for a long while; then he rolled over on his side, wound his watch, and lay there until morning.

Another day of fog. Half of his last blanket had gone into foot-wrappings. He failed to pick up Bill's trail. It did not matter. His hunger was driving him too compellingly—only—only he wondered if Bill, too, were lost. By midday the irk of his pack became too oppressive. Again he divided the gold, this time merely spilling half of it on the ground. In the afternoon he threw the rest of it away, there remaining to him only the half-blanket, the tin bucket, and the rifle.

An hallucination began to trouble him. He felt confident that one cartridge remained to him. It was in the chamber of the rifle and he had overlooked it. On the other hand, he knew all the time that the chamber was empty. But the hallucination persisted. He fought it off for hours, then threw his rifle open and was confronted with emptiness. The disappointment was as bitter as though he had really expected to find the cartridge.

He plodded on for half an hour, when the hallucination arose again. Again he fought it, and still it persisted, till for very relief he opened his rifle to unconvince himself. At times his mind wandered farther afield, and he plodded on, a mere automaton, strange conceits and whimsicalities gnawing at his brain like worms. But these excursions out of the real were of brief duration, for ever the pangs of the hunger-bite called him back. He was jerked back abruptly once from such an excursion by a sight that caused him nearly to faint. He reeled and swayed, doddering like a drunken man to keep from falling. Before him stood a horse. A horse! He could not believe his eyes. A thick mist was in them, intershot with sparkling points of light. He rubbed his eyes savagely to clear his vision, and beheld, not a horse, but a great brown bear. The animal was studying him with bellicose curiosity.

The man had brought his gun halfway to his shoulder before he realized. He lowered it and drew his hunting-knife from its beaded sheath at his hip. Before him was meat and life. He ran his thumb along the edge of his knife. It was sharp. The point was sharp. He would fling himself upon the bear and kill it. But his heart began its warning thump, thump, thump. Then followed the wild upward leap and tattoo of flutters, the pressing as of an iron band about his forehead, the creeping of the dizziness into his brain.

His desperate courage was evicted by a great surge of fear. In his weakness, what if the animal attacked him? He drew himself up to his most imposing stature, gripping the knife and staring hard at the bear. The bear advanced clumsily a couple of steps, reared up, and gave vent to a tentative growl. If the man ran, he would run after him; but the man did not run. He was animated now with the courage of fear. He, too, growled, savagely, terribly, voicing the fear that is to life germane and that lies twisted about life's deepest roots.

The bear edged away to one side, growling menacingly, himself appalled by this mysterious creature that appeared upright and unafraid. But the man did not move. He stood like a statue till the danger was past, when he yielded to a fit of trembling and sank down into the wet moss.

He pulled himself together and went on, afraid now in a new way. It was not the fear that he should die passively from lack of food, but that he should be destroyed violently before starvation had exhausted the last particle of the endeavor in him that made toward surviving. There were the wolves. Back and forth across the desolation drifted their howls, weaving the very air into a fabric of menace that was so tangible that he found himself, arms in the air, pressing it back from him as it might be the walls of a wind-blown tent.

Now and again the wolves, in packs of two and three, crossed his path. But they steered clear of him. They were not in sufficient numbers, and besides, they were hunting the caribou, which did not battle, while this strange creature that walked erect might scratch and bite.

In the late afternoon he came upon scattered bones where the wolves had made a kill. The débris had been a caribou calf an hour before, squawking and running and very much alive. He contemplated the bones, clean-picked and polished, pink with the cell-life in them which had not yet died. Could it possibly be that he might be that ere the day was done! Such was life, eh? A vain and fleeting thing. It was only life that pained. There was no hurt in death. To die was to sleep. It meant cessation, rest. Then why was he not content to die?

But he did not moralize long. He was squatting in the moss, a bone in his mouth, sucking at the shreds of life that still dyed it faintly pink. The sweet meaty taste, thin and elusive almost as a memory, maddened him. He closed his jaws on the bones and crunched. Sometimes it was the bone that broke, sometimes his teeth. Then he crushed the bones between rocks, pounded them to a pulp, and swallowed them. He pounded his fingers, too, in his haste, and yet found a moment in which to feel surprise at the fact that his fingers did not hurt much when caught under the descending rock.

Came frightful days of snow and rain. He did not know when he made camp, when he broke camp. He travelled in the night as much as in the day. He rested wherever he fell, crawled on whenever the dying life in him flickered up and burned less dimly. He, as a man, no longer strove. It was the life in him, unwilling to die, that drove him on. He did not suffer. His nerves had become blunted, numb, while his mind was filled with weird visions and delicious dreams.

But ever he sucked and chewed on the crushed bones of the caribou calf, the least remnants of which he had gathered up and carried with him. He crossed no more hills or divides, but automatically followed a large stream which flowed through a wide and shallow valley. He did not see this stream nor this valley. He saw nothing save visions. Soul and body walked or crawled side by side, yet apart, so slender was the thread that bound them.

He awoke in his right mind, lying on his back on a rocky ledge. The sun was shining bright and warm. Afar off he heard the squawking of caribou calves. He was aware of vague memories of rain and wind and snow, but whether he had been beaten by the storm for two days or two weeks he did not know. For some time he lay without movement, the genial sunshine pouring upon him and saturating his miserable body with its warmth. A fine day, he thought. Perhaps he could manage to locate himself. By a painful effort he rolled over on his side. Below him flowed a wide and sluggish river. Its unfamiliarity puzzled him. Slowly he followed it with his eyes, winding in wide sweeps among the bleak, bare hills, bleaker and barer and lower-lying than any hills he had yet encountered. Slowly, deliberately, without excitement or more than the most casual interest, he followed the course of the strange stream toward the sky-line and saw it emptying into a bright and shining sea. He was still unexcited. Most unusual, he thought, a vision or a mirage—more likely a vision, a trick of his disordered mind. He was confirmed in this by sight of a ship lying at anchor in the midst of the shining sea. He closed his eyes for a while, then opened them. Strange how the vision persisted! Yet not strange. He knew there were no seas or ships in the heart of the barren lands, just as he had known there was no cartridge in the empty rifle.

He heard a snuffle behind him—a half-choking gasp or cough. Very slowly, because of his exceeding weakness and stiffness, he rolled over on his other side. He could see nothing near at hand, but he waited patiently. Again came the snuffle and cough, and outlined between two jagged rocks not a score of feet away he made out the gray head of a wolf. The sharp ears were not pricked so sharply as he had seen them on other wolves; the eyes were bleared and bloodshot, the head seemed to droop limply and forlornly. The animal blinked continually in the sunshine. It seemed sick. As he looked it snuffled and coughed again.

This, at least, was real, he thought, and turned on the other side so that he might see the reality of the world which had been veiled from him before by the vision. But the sea still shone in the distance and the ship was plainly discernible. Was it reality, after all? He closed his eyes for a long while and thought, and then it came to him. He had been making north by east, away from the Dease Divide and into the Coppermine Valley. This wide and sluggish river was the Coppermine. That shining sea was the Arctic Ocean. That ship was a whaler, strayed east, far east, from the mouth of the Mackenzie, and it was lying at anchor in Coronation Gulf. He remembered the Hudson Bay Company chart he had seen long ago, and it was all clear and reasonable to him.

He sat up and turned his attention to immediate affairs. He had worn through the blanket-wrappings, and his feet were shapeless lumps of raw meat. His last blanket was gone. Rifle and knife were both missing. He had lost his hat somewhere, with the bunch of matches in the band, but the matches against his chest were safe and dry inside the tobacco pouch and oil paper. He looked at his watch. It marked eleven o'clock and was still running. Evidently he had kept it wound.

He was calm and collected. Though extremely weak, he had no sensation of pain. He was not hungry. The thought of food was not even pleasant to him, and whatever he did was done by reason alone. He ripped off his pants' legs to the knees and bound them about his feet. Somehow he had succeeded in retaining the tin bucket. He would have some hot water before he began what he foresaw was to be a terrible journey to the ship.

His movements were slow. He shook as with a palsy. When he started to collect dry moss, he found he could not rise to his feet. He tried again and again, then contented himself with crawling about on hands and knees. Once he crawled near to the sick wolf. The animal dragged itself reluctantly out of his way, licking its chops with a tongue which seemed hardly to have the strength to curl. The man noticed that tongue was not the customary healthy red. It was a yellowish brown and seemed coated with a rough and half-dry mucus.

After he had drunk a quart of hot water the man found he was able to stand, and even to walk as well as a dying man might be supposed to walk. Every minute or so he was compelled to rest. His steps were feeble and uncertain, just as the wolf's that trailed him were feeble and uncertain; and that night, when the shining sea was blotted out by blackness, he knew he was nearer to it by no more than four miles.

Throughout the night he heard the cough of the sick wolf, and now and then the squawking of the caribou calves. There was life all around him, but it was strong life, very much alive and well, and he knew the sick wolf clung to the sick man's trail in the hope that the man would die first. In the morning, on opening his eyes, he beheld it regarding him with a wistful and hungry stare. It stood crouched, with tail between its legs, like a miserable and woe-begone dog. It shivered in the chill morning wind, and grinned dispiritedly when the man spoke to it in a voice that achieved no more than a hoarse whisper.

The sun rose brightly, and all morning the man tottered and fell toward the ship on the shining sea. The weather was perfect. It was the brief Indian Summer of the high latitudes. It might last a week. To-morrow or next day it might be gone.

In the afternoon the man came upon a trail. It was of another man, who did not walk, but who dragged himself on all fours. The man thought it might be Bill, but he thought in a dull, uninterested way. He had no curiosity. In fact, sensation and emotion had left him. He was no longer susceptible to pain. Stomach and nerves had gone to sleep. Yet the life that was in him drove him on. He was very weary, but it refused to die. It was because it refused to die that he still ate muskeg berries and minnows, drank his hot water, and kept a wary eye on the sick wolf.

He followed the trail of the other man who dragged himself along, and soon came to the end of it—a few fresh-picked bones where the soggy moss was marked by the foot-pads of many wolves. He saw a squat moose-hide sack, mate to his own, which had been torn by sharp teeth. He picked it up, though its weight was almost too much for his feeble fingers. Bill had carried it to the last. Ha! ha! He would have the laugh on Bill. He would survive and carry it to the ship in the shining sea. His mirth was hoarse and ghastly, like a raven's croak, and the sick wolf joined him, howling lugubriously. The man ceased suddenly. How could he have the laugh on Bill if that were Bill; if those bones, so pinky-white and clean, were Bill?

He turned away. Well, Bill had deserted him; but he would not take the gold, nor would he suck Bill's bones. Bill would have, though, had it been the other way around, he mused as he staggered on.

He came to a pool of water. Stooping over in quest of minnows, he jerked his head back as though he had been stung. He had caught sight of his reflected face. So horrible was it that sensibility awoke long enough to be shocked. There were three minnows in the pool, which was too large to drain; and after several ineffectual attempts to catch them in the tin bucket he forbore. He was afraid, because of his great weakness, that he might fall in and drown. It was for this reason that he did not trust himself to the river astride one of the many drift-logs which lined its sand-spits.

That day he decreased the distance between him and the ship by three miles; the next day by two—for he was crawling now as Bill had crawled; and the end of the fifth day found the ship still seven miles away and him unable to make even a mile a day. Still the Indian Summer held on, and he continued to crawl and faint, turn and turn about; and ever the sick wolf coughed and wheezed at his heels. His knees had become raw meat like his feet, and though he padded them with the shirt from his back it was a red track he left behind him on the moss and stones. Once, glancing back, he saw the wolf licking hungrily his bleeding trail, and he saw sharply what his own end might be—unless—unless he could get the wolf. Then began as grim a tragedy of existence as was ever played—a sick man that crawled, a sick wolf that limped, two creatures dragging their dying carcasses across the desolation and hunting each other's lives.

Had it been a well wolf, it would not have mattered so much to the man; but the thought of going to feed the maw of that loathsome and all but dead thing was repugnant to him. He was finicky. His mind had begun to wander again, and to be perplexed by hallucinations, while his lucid intervals grew rarer and shorter.

He was awakened once from a faint by a wheeze close in his ear. The wolf leaped lamely back, losing its footing and falling in its weakness. It was ludicrous, but he was not amused. Nor was he even afraid. He was too far gone for that. But his mind was for the moment clear, and he lay and considered. The ship was no more than four miles away. He could see it quite distinctly when he rubbed the mists out of his eyes, and he could see the white sail of a small boat cutting the water of the shining sea. But he could never crawl those four miles. He knew that, and was very calm in the knowledge. He knew that he could not crawl half a mile. And yet he wanted to live. It was unreasonable that he should die after all he had undergone. Fate asked too much of him. And, dying, he declined to die. It was stark madness, perhaps, but in the very grip of Death he defied Death and refused to die.

He closed his eyes and composed himself with infinite precaution. He steeled himself to keep above the suffocating languor that lapped like a rising tide through all the wells of his being. It was very like a sea, this deadly languor, that rose and rose and drowned his consciousness bit by bit. Sometimes he was all but submerged, swimming through oblivion with a faltering stroke; and again, by some strange alchemy of soul, he would find another shred of will and strike out more strongly.

Without movement he lay on his back, and he could hear, slowly drawing near and nearer, the wheezing intake and output of the sick wolf's breath. It drew closer, ever closer, through an infinitude of time, and he did not move. It was at his ear. The harsh dry tongue grated like sandpaper against his cheek. His hands shot out—or at least he willed them to shoot out. The fingers were curved like talons, but they closed on empty air. Swiftness and certitude require strength, and the man had not this strength.

The patience of the wolf was terrible. The man's patience was no less terrible. For half a day he lay motionless, fighting off unconsciousness and waiting for the thing that was to feed upon him and upon which he wished to feed. Sometimes the languid sea rose over him and he dreamed long dreams; but ever through it all, waking and dreaming, he waited for the wheezing breath and the harsh caress of the tongue.

He did not hear the breath, and he slipped slowly from some dream to the feel of the tongue along his hand. He waited. The fangs pressed softly; the pressure increased; the wolf was exerting its last strength in an effort to sink teeth in the food for which it had waited so long. But the man had waited long, and the lacerated hand closed on the jaw. Slowly, while the wolf struggled feebly and the hand clutched feebly, the other hand crept across to a grip. Five minutes later the whole weight of the man's body was on top of the wolf. The hands had not sufficient strength to choke the wolf, but the face of the man was pressed close to the throat of the wolf and the mouth of the man was full of hair. At the end of half an hour the man was aware of a warm trickle in his throat. It was not pleasant. It was like molten lead being forced into his stomach, and it was forced by his will alone. Later the man rolled over on his back and slept.

There were some members of a scientific expedition on the whale-ship *Bedford*. From the deck they remarked a strange object on the shore. It was moving down the beach toward the water. They were unable to classify it, and, being scientific men, they climbed into the whale-boat alongside and went ashore to see. And they saw something that was alive but which could hardly be called a man. It was blind, unconscious. It squirmed along the ground like some monstrous worm. Most of its efforts were ineffectual, but it was persistent, and it writhed and twisted and went ahead perhaps a score of feet an hour.

Three weeks afterward the man lay in a bunk on the whale-ship *Bedford*, and with tears streaming down his wasted cheeks told who he was and what he had undergone. He also babbled incoherently of his mother, of sunny Southern California, and a home among the orange groves and flowers.

The days were not many after that when he sat at table with the scientific men and ship's officers. He gloated over the spectacle of so much food, watching it anxiously as it went into the mouths of others. With the disappearance of each mouthful an expression of deep regret came into his eyes. He was quite sane, yet he hated those men at meal-time. He was haunted by a fear that the food would not last. He inquired of the cook, the cabin-boy, the captain, concerning the food stores. They reassured him countless times; but he could not believe them, and pried cunningly about the lazarette to see with his own eyes.

It was noticed that the man was getting fat. He grew stouter with each day. The scientific men shook their heads and theorized. They limited the man at his meals, but still his girth increased and he swelled prodigiously under his shirt.

The sailors grinned. They knew. And when the scientific men set a watch on the man, they knew too. They saw him slouch for'ard after breakfast, and, like a mendicant, with outstretched palm, accost a sailor. The sailor grinned and passed him a fragment of sea biscuit. He clutched it avariciously, looked at it as a miser looks at gold, and thrust it into his shirt bosom. Similar were the donations from other grinning sailors.

The scientific men were discreet. They let him alone. But they privily examined his bunk. It was lined with hardtack; the mattress was stuffed with hardtack; every nook and cranny was filled with hardtack.

Yet he was sane. He was taking precautions against another possible famine—that was all. He would recover from it, the scientific men said, and he did, ere the *Bedford*'s anchor rumbled down in San Francisco Bay.

11

AN ADVENTURE WITH A DOG AND A GLACIER

BY JOHN MUIR

Depending on a dog to make your escape from a deadly wilderness trap isn't a likely choice for survival, but that is exactly what happened to John Muir, one of America's most distinguished naturalist authors. Muir (1838–1914) wrote engaging accounts of his travels among the mountain peaks of the American West and Alaska. This tale is typical bonded Muir and is from his Travels in Alaska *(1915).*

In the summer of 1880 I set out from Fort Wrangel in a canoe, with the Rev. S. H. Young, my former companion, and a crew of Indians, to continue the exploration of the icy region of southeastern Alaska, begun in the fall of 1879. After the necessary provisions, blankets, etc., had been collected and stowed away, and the Indians were in their places ready to dip their paddles, while a crowd of their friends were looking down from the wharf to bid them good-by and good luck, Mr. Young, for whom we were waiting, at length came aboard, followed by a little black dog that immediately made himself at home by curling up in a hollow among the baggage. I like dogs, but this one seemed so small, dull, and worthless that I objected to his going, and asked the missionary why he was taking him. "Such a helpless wisp of hair will only be in the way," I said. "You had better pass him up to one of the Indian boys on the wharf, to be taken home to play with the children. This trip is not likely to be a good one for toy dogs. He will be rained on and snowed on for weeks, and will require care like a baby." But the missionary assured me that he would be no trouble at all; that he was a perfect wonder of a dog—could endure cold and hunger like a polar bear, could swim like a seal, and was wondrous wise, etc., making out a list of virtues likely to make him the most interesting of the company.

Nobody could hope to unravel the lines of his ancestry. He was short-legged, bunchy-bodied, and almost featureless—something like a muskrat. Though smooth, his hair was long and silky, so that when the wind was at his back it ruffled, making him look shaggy. At first sight his only noticeable feature was his showy tail, which was about as shady and airy as a squirrel's, and was carried curling forward nearly to his ears. On closer inspection you might see his thin, sensitive ears and his keen dark eye with cunning tan spots. Mr. Young told me that when the dog was about the size of a wood-rat he was presented to his wife by an Irish prospector at Sitka, and that when he arrived at Fort Wrangel he was adopted by the Stickeen Indians as a sort of new good-luck totem, and named "Stickeen" for the tribe, with whom he became a favorite.

On our trip he soon proved himself a queer character—odd, concealed, independent, keeping invincibly quiet, and doing many inexplicable things that piqued my curiosity. Sailing week after week through the long, intricate channels and inlets among the innumerable islands and mountains of the coast, he spent the dull days in sluggish ease, motionless, and apparently as unobserving as a hibernating marmot. But I discovered that somehow he always knew what was going forward. When the Indians were about to shoot at ducks or seals, or when anything interesting was to be seen along the shore, he would rest his chin on the edge of the canoe and calmly look out. When he heard us talking about making a landing, he roused himself to see what sort of place we were coming to, and made ready to jump overboard and swim ashore as soon as the canoe neared the beach. Then, with a vigorous shake to get rid of the brine in his hair, he went into the woods to hunt small game.

But though always the first out of the canoe, he was always the last to get into it. When we were ready to start he could never be found, and refused to come to our call. We soon found out, however, that though we could not see him at such times, he saw us, and from the cover of the briers and huckleberry-bushes in the fringe of the woods was watching the canoe with wary eye. For as soon as we were fairly off, he came trotting down the beach, plunged into the surf, and swam after us, knowing well that we would cease rowing and take him in. When the contrary little vagabond came alongside, he was lifted by the neck, held at arm's length a moment to drip, and dropped aboard. We tried to cure him of this trick by compelling him to swim farther before stopping for him; but this did no good: the longer the swim, the better he seemed to like it.

Though capable of most spacious idleness, he was always ready for excursions or adventures of any sort. When the Indians went into the woods for a deer, Stickeen was sure to be at their heels, provided I had not yet left camp. For though I never carried a gun, he always followed me, forsaking the hunting Indians, and even his master, to share my wanderings. The days that were too stormy for sailing I spent in the woods, or on the mountains or glaciers, wherever I chanced to be; and Stickeen always insisted on following me, gliding through the dripping huckleberry-bushes and prickly Panax and Rubus tangles like a fox, scarce stirring their close-set branches, wading and wallowing through snow, swimming ice-cold streams, jumping logs and rocks and the crusty hummocks and crevasses of glaciers with the patience and endurance of a determined mountaineer, never tiring or getting discouraged. Once he followed me over a glacier the surface of which was so rough that it cut his feet until every step was marked with blood; but he trotted on with Indian fortitude until I noticed his pain and, taking pity on him, made him a set of moccasins out of a handkerchief. But he never asked help or made any complaint, as if, like a philosopher, he had learned that without hard work and suffering there could be no pleasure worth having.

Yet nobody knew what Stickeen was good for. He seemed to meet danger and hardships without reason, insisted on having his own way, never obeyed an order, and the hunters could never set him on anything against his will, or make him fetch anything that was shot. I tried hard to make his acquaintance, guessing there must be something in him; but he was as cold as a glacier, and about as invulnerable to fun, though his master assured me that he played at home, and in some measure conformed to the usages of civilization. His equanimity was so immovable it seemed due to unfeeling ignorance. Let the weather blow and roar, he was as tranquil as a stone; and no matter what advances you made, scarce a glance or a tail-wag would you get for your pains. No superannuated mastiff or bulldog grown old in office surpassed this soft midget in stoic dignity. He sometimes reminded me of those plump, squat, unshakable cacti of the Arizona deserts that give no sign of feeling. A true child of the wilderness, holding the even tenor of his hidden life with the silence and serenity of nature, he never displayed a trace of the elfish vivacity and fun of the terriers and collies that we all know, nor of their touching affection and devotion. Like children, most small dogs beg to be loved and allowed to love, but Stickeen seemed a very Diogenes, asking only to be let alone. He seemed neither old nor young. His strength lay in his eyes. They looked as old as the hills, and as young and as wild. I never tired looking into them. It was like looking into a landscape; but they were small and rather deep-set, and had no explaining puckers around them to give out particulars. I was accustomed to look into the faces of plants and animals, and I watched the little sphinx more and more keenly as an interesting study. But there is no estimating the wit and wisdom concealed and latent in our lower fellow-mortals until made manifest by profound experiences; for it is by suffering that dogs as well as saints are developed and made perfect.

After we had explored the glaciers of the Sumdum and Tahkoo inlets, we sailed through Stephen's Passage into Lynn Canal, and thence through Icy Strait into Cross Sound, looking for unexplored inlets leading toward the ice-fountains of the Fairweather Range. While the tide was in our favor in Cross Sound we were accompanied by a fleet of icebergs drifting out to the ocean from Glacier Bay. Slowly we crawled around Vancouver's Point, *Wimbledon*, our frail canoe, tossed like a feather on the massive swells coming in past Cape Spenser. For miles the Sound is bounded by precipitous cliffs which looked terribly stern in gloomy weather. Had our canoe been crushed or upset, we could have gained no landing here; for the cliffs, as high as those of Yosemite, sink perfectly sheer into deep water. Eagerly we scanned the immense wall on the north side for the first sign of an opening, all of us anxious except Stickeen, who dozed in peace or gazed dreamily at the tremendous precipices when he heard us talking about them. At length we discovered the entrance of what is now called Taylor Bay, and about five o'clock reached the head of it, and encamped near the front of a large glacier which extends as an abrupt barrier all the way across from wall to wall of the inlet, a distance of three or four miles.

On first observation the glacier presented some unusual features, and that night I planned a grand excursion for the morrow. I awoke early, called not only by the glacier, but also by a storm. Rain, mixed with trailing films of scud and the ragged, drawn-out nether surfaces of gray clouds, filled the inlet, and was sweeping forward in a thick, passionate, horizontal flood, as if it were all passing over the country instead of falling on it. Everything was streaming with life and motion—woods, rocks, waters, and the sky. The main perennial streams were booming, and hundreds of new ones, born of the rain, were descending in gray and white cascades on each side of the inlet, fairly streaking their rocky slopes, and roaring like the sea. I had intended making a cup of coffee before starting, but when I heard the storm I made haste to join it; for in storms nature has always something extra fine to show us, and if we have wit to keep in right relations with them the danger is no more than in home-keeping, and we can go with them rejoicing, sharing their enthusiasm, and chanting with the old Norsemen, "The blast of the tempest aids our oars; the hurricane is our servant, and drives us whither we wish to go."

So I took my ice-ax, buttoned my coat, put a piece of bread in my pocket, and set out. Mr. Young and the Indians were asleep, and so, I hoped, was Stickeen; but I had not gone a dozen rods before he left his warm bed in the tent, and came boring through the blast after me. That a man should welcome storms for their exhilarating music and motion, and go forth to see God making landscapes, is reasonable enough; but what fascination could there be in dismal weather for this poor, feeble wisp of a dog, so pathetically small? Anyhow, on he came, breakfastless, through the choking blast. I stopped, turned my back to the wind, and gave him a good, dissuasive talk. "Now don't," I said, shouting to make myself heard in the storm—"now don't, Stickeen. What has got into your queer noddle now? You must be daft. This wild day has nothing for you. Go back to camp and keep warm. There is no game abroad—nothing but weather. Not a foot or wing is stirring. Wait and get a good breakfast with your master, and be sensible for once. I can't feed you or carry you, and this storm will kill you."

But nature, it seems, was at the bottom of the affair; and she gains her ends with dogs as well as with men, making us do as she likes, driving us on her ways, however rough. So after ordering him back again and again to ease my conscience, I saw that he was not to be shaken off; as well might the earth try to shake off the moon. I had once led his master into trouble, when he fell on one of the topmost jags of a mountain, and dislocated his arms. Now the turn of his humble companion was coming. The dog just stood there in the wind, drenched and blinking, saying doggedly, "Where thou goest I will go." So I told him to come on, if he must, and gave him a piece of the bread I had put in my pocket for breakfast. Then we pushed on in company, and thus began the most memorable of all my wild days.

The level flood, driving straight in our faces, thrashed and washed us wildly until we got into the shelter of the trees and ice-cliffs on the east side of the glacier, where we rested and listened and looked on in comfort. The exploration of the glacier was my main object, but the wind was too high to allow excursions over its open surface, where one might be dangerously shoved while balancing for a jump on the brink of a crevasse. In the meantime the storm was a fine study. Here the end of the glacier, descending over an abrupt swell of resisting rock about five hundred feet high, leans forward and falls in majestic ice-cascades. And as the storm came down the glacier from the north, Stickeen and I were beneath the main current of the blast, while favorably located to see and hear it. A broad torrent, draining the side of the glacier, now swollen by scores of new streams from the mountains, was rolling boulders along its rocky channel between the glacier and the woods with thudding, bumping, muffled sounds, rushing toward the bay with tremendous energy, as if in haste to get out of the mountains, the waters above and beneath calling to each other, and all to the ocean, their home. Looking southward from our shelter, we had this great torrent on our left, with mossy woods on the mountain slope above it, the glacier on our right, the wild, cascading portion of it forming a multitude of towers, spires, and flat-topped battlements seen through the trees, and smooth gray gloom ahead. I tried to draw the marvelous scene in my note-book, but the rain fell on my page in spite of all that I could do to shelter it, and the sketch seemed miserably defective.

When the wind began to abate I traced the east side of the glacier. All the trees standing on the edge of the woods were barked and bruised, showing high ice-mark in a very telling way, while tens of thousands of those that had stood for centuries on the bank of the glacier farther out lay crushed and being crushed. In many places I could see, down fifty feet or so beneath, the margin of the glacier mill, where trunks from one to two feet in diameter were being ground to pulp against outstanding rock-ribs and bosses of the bank. About three miles above the front of the glacier, I climbed to the surface of it by means of ax-steps, made easy for Stickeen; and as far as the eye could reach, the level, or nearly level, glacier stretched away indefinitely beneath the gray sky, a seemingly boundless prairie of ice. The rain continued, which I did not mind; but a tendency to fogginess in the drooping clouds made me hesitate about venturing far from land. No trace of the west shore was visible, and in case the misty clouds should settle, or the wind again become violent, I feared getting caught in a tangle of crevasses.

Lingering undecided, watching the weather, I sauntered about on the crystal sea. For a mile or two out I found the ice remarkably safe. The marginal crevasses were mostly narrow, while the few wider ones were easily avoided by passing around them, and the clouds began to open here and there. Thus encouraged, I at last pushed out for the other side; for nature can make us do anything she likes, luring us along appointed ways for the fulfillment of her plans.

At first we made rapid progress, and the sky was not very threatening, while I took bearings occasionally with a pocket-compass, to enable me to retrace my way more surely in case the storm should become blinding; but the structure-lines of the ice were my main guide. Toward the west side we came to a closely crevassed section, in which we had to make long, narrow tacks and doublings, tracing the edges of tremendous longitudinal crevasses, many of which were from twenty to thirty feet wide, and perhaps a thousand feet deep, beautiful and awful. In working a way through them I was severely cautious, but Stickeen came on as unhesitatingly as the flying clouds. Any crevasse that I could jump he would leap without so much as halting to examine it.

The weather was bright and dark, with quick flashes of summer and winter close together. When the clouds opened and the sun shone, the glacier was seen from shore to shore, with a bright array of encompassing mountains partly revealed, wearing the clouds as garments, black in the middle, burning on the edges, and the whole icy prairie seemed to burst into a bloom of iris colors from myriads of crystals. Then suddenly all the glorious show would be again smothered in gloom. But Stickeen seemed to care for none of these things, bright or dark, nor for the beautiful wells filled to the brim with water so pure that it was nearly invisible, the rumbling, grinding moulins, or the quick-flashing, glinting, swirling streams in frictionless channels of living ice. Nothing seemed novel to him. He showed neither caution nor curiosity. His courage was so unwavering that it seemed due to dullness of perception, as if he were only blindly bold; and I warned him that he might slip or fall short. His bunchy body seemed all one skipping muscle, and his peg legs appeared to be jointed only at the top.

We gained the west shore in about three hours, the width of the glacier here being about seven miles. Then I pushed northward, in order to see as far back as possible into the fountains of the Fairweather Mountains, in case the clouds should rise. The walking was easy along the margin of the forest, which, of course, like that on the other side, had been invaded and crushed by the swollen glacier. In an hour we rounded a massive headland and came suddenly on another outlet of the glacier, which, in the form of a wild ice-cascade, was pouring over the rim of the main basin toward the ocean with the volume of a thousand Niagaras. The surface was broken into a multitude of sharp blades and pinnacles leaning forward, something like the updashing waves of a flood of water descending a rugged channel. But these ice-waves were many times higher than those of river cataracts, and to all appearance motionless. It was a dazzling white torrent two miles wide, flowing between high banks black with trees. Tracing its left bank three or four miles, I found that it discharged into a freshwater lake, filling it with icebergs.

I would gladly have followed the outlet, but the day was waning, and we had to make haste on the return trip to get off the ice before dark. When we were about two miles from the west shore the clouds dropped misty fringes, and snow soon began to fly. Then I began to feel anxiety as to finding a way in the storm through the intricate network of crevasses which we had entered. Stickeen showed no fear. He was still the same silent, sufficient, uncomplaining Indian philosopher. When the storm-darkness fell he kept close behind me. The snow warned us to make haste, but at the same time hid our way. At rare intervals the clouds thinned, and mountains, looming in the gloom, frowned and quickly vanished.

I pushed on as best I could, jumping innumerable crevasses, and for every hundred rods or so of direct advance traveling a mile in doubling up and down in the turmoil of chasms and dislocated masses of ice. After an hour or two of this work we came to a series of longitudinal crevasses of appalling width, like immense furrows. These I traced with firm nerve, excited and strengthened by the danger, making wide jumps, poising cautiously on the dizzy edges after cutting hollows for my feet before making the spring, to avoid slipping or any uncertainty on the farther sides, where only one trial is granted— exercise at once frightful and inspiring. Stickeen flirted across every gap I jumped, seemingly without effort. Many a mile we thus traveled, mostly up and down, making but little real headway in crossing, most of the time running instead of walking, as the danger of spending the night on the glacier became threatening. No doubt we could have weathered the storm for one night, and I faced the chance of being compelled to do so; but we were hungry and wet, and the north wind was thick with snow and bitterly cold, and of course that night would have seemed a long one. Stickeen gave me no concern. He was still the wonderful, inscrutable philosopher, ready for anything. I could not see far enough to judge in which direction the best route lay, and had simply to grope my way in the snow-choked air and ice. Again and again I was put to my mettle, but Stickeen followed easily, his nerves growing more unflinching as the dangers thickened; so it always is with mountaineers.

At length our way was barred by a very wide and straight crevasse, which I traced rapidly northward a mile or so without finding a crossing or hope of one, then southward down the glacier about as far, to where it united with another crevasse. In all this distance of perhaps two miles there was only one place where I could possibly jump it; but the width of this jump was nearly the utmost I dared attempt, while the danger of slipping on the farther side was so great that I was loath to try it. Furthermore, the side I was on was about a foot higher than the other, and even with this advantage it seemed dangerously wide. One is liable to underestimate the width of crevasses where the magnitudes in general are great. I therefore measured this one again and again, until satisfied that I could jump it if necessary, but that in case I should be compelled to jump back to the higher side, I might fail.

Now a cautious mountaineer seldom takes a step on unknown ground which seems at all dangerous, that he cannot retrace in case he should be stopped by unseen obstacles ahead. This is the rule of mountaineers who live long; and though in haste, I compelled myself to sit down and deliberate before I broke it. Retracing my devious path in imagination, as if it were drawn on a chart, I saw that I was recrossing the glacier a mile or two farther up-stream, and was entangled in a section I had not before seen. Should I risk this dangerous jump, or try to regain the woods on the west shore, make a fire, and have only hunger to endure while waiting for a new day? I had already crossed so broad a tangle of dangerous ice that I saw it would be difficult to get back to the woods through the storm; while the ice just beyond the present barrier seemed more promising, and the east shore was now perhaps about as near as the west. I was therefore eager to go on; but this wide jump was a tremendous obstacle.

At length, because of the dangers already behind me, I determined to venture against those that might be ahead, jumped, and landed well, but with so little to spare that I more than ever dreaded being compelled to take that jump back from the lower side. Stickeen followed, making nothing of it. But within a distance of a few hundred yards we were stopped again by the widest crevasse yet encountered. Of course I made haste to explore it, hoping all might yet be well. About three fourths of a mile up-stream it united with the one we had just crossed, as I feared it would. Then, tracing it down, I found it joined the other great crevasse at the lower end, maintaining a width of forty to fifty feet. We were on an island about two miles long and from one hundred to three hundred yards wide, with two barely possible ways of escape—one by the way we came, the other by an almost inaccessible sliver-bridge that crossed the larger crevasse from near the middle of the island.

After tracing the brink, I ran back to the sliver-bridge and cautiously studied it. Crevasses caused by strains from variations of the rate of motion of different parts of the glacier and by convexities in the channel are mere cracks when they first open—so narrow as hardly to admit the blade of a pocket-knife—and widen gradually, according to the extent of the strain. Now some of these cracks are interrupted like the cracks in wood, and, in opening, the strip of ice between overlapping ends is dragged out; and if the flow of the glacier there is such that no strain is made on the sliver, it maintains a continuous connection between the sides, just as the two sides of a slivered crack in wood that is being split are connected. Some crevasses remain open for years, and by the melting of their sides continue to increase in width long after the opening strain has ceased, while the sliver-bridges, level on top at first, and perfectly safe, are at length melted to thin, knife-edged blades, the upper portion being most exposed to the weather; and since the exposure is greatest in the middle, they at length curve downward like the cables of suspension-bridges.

This one was evidently very old, for it had been wasted until it was the worst bridge I ever saw. The width of the crevasse was here about fifty feet, and the sliver, crossing diagonally, was about seventy feet long, was depressed twenty-five or thirty feet in the middle, and the up-curving ends were attached to the sides eight or ten feet below the surface of the glacier. Getting down the nearly vertical wall to the end of it and up the other side were the main difficulties, and they seemed all but insurmountable. Of the many perils encountered in my years of wandering in mountain altitudes, none seemed so plain and stern and merciless as this. And it was presented when we were wet to the skin and hungry, the sky was dark with snow, and the night near, and we had to fear the snow in our eyes and the disturbing action of the wind in any movement we might make. But we were forced to face it. It was a tremendous necessity.

Beginning not immediately above the sunken end of the bridge, but a little to one side, I cut nice hollows on the brink for my knees to rest in; then, leaning over, with my short-handled ax cut a step sixteen or eighteen inches below, which, on account of the sheerness of the wall, was shallow. That step, however, was well made; its floor sloped slightly inward, and formed a good hold for my heels. Then, slipping cautiously upon it, and crouching as low as possible, with my left side twisted toward the wall, I steadied myself with my left hand in a slight notch, while with the right I cut other steps and notches in succession, guarding against glinting of the ax, for life or death was in every stroke, and in the niceness of finish of every foothold.

After the end of the bridge was reached, it was a delicate thing to poise on a little platform which I had chipped on its up-curving end, and, bending over the slippery surface, get astride of it. Crossing was easy, cutting off the sharp edge with careful strokes, and hitching forward a few inches at a time, keeping my balance with my knees pressed against its sides. The tremendous abyss on each side I studiously ignored. The surface of that blue sliver was then all the world. But the most trying part of the adventure was, after working my way across inch by inch, to rise from the safe position astride that slippery strip of ice, and to cut a ladder in the face of the wall—chipping, climbing, holding on with feet and fingers in mere notches. At such times one's whole body is eye, and common skill and fortitude are replaced by power beyond our call or knowledge. Never before had I been so long under deadly strain. How I got up the cliff at the end of the bridge I never could tell. The thing seemed to have been done by somebody else. I never have had contempt of death, though in the course of my explorations I oftentimes felt that to meet one's fate on a mountain, in a grand cañon, or in the heart of a crystal glacier would be blessed as compared with death from disease, a mean accident in a street, or from a sniff of sewer-gas. But the sweetest, cleanest death, set thus calmly and glaringly clear before us, is hard enough to face, even though we feel gratefully sure that we have already had happiness enough for a dozen lives.

But poor Stickeen, the wee, silky, sleekit beastie—think of him! When I had decided to try the bridge, and while I was on my knees cutting away the rounded brow, he came behind me, pushed his head past my shoulder, looked down and across, scanned the sliver and its approaches with his queer eyes, then looked me in the face with a startled air of surprise and concern, and began to mutter and whine, saying as plainly as if speaking with words, "Surely you are not going to try that awful place?" This was the first time I had seen him gaze deliberately into a crevasse or into my face with a speaking look. That he should have recognized and appreciated the danger at the first glance showed wonderful sagacity. Never before had the quick, daring midget seemed to know that ice was slippery, or that there was such a thing as danger anywhere. His looks and the tones of his voice when he began to complain and speak his fears were so human that I unconsciously talked to him as I would to a boy, and in trying to calm his fears perhaps in some measure moderated my own.

"Hush your fears, my boy," I said. "We will get across safe, though it is not going to be easy. No right way is easy in this rough world. We must risk our lives to save them. At the worst we can only slip; and then how grand a grave we shall have! And by and by our nice bones will do good in the terminal moraine."

But my sermon was far from reassuring him; he began to cry, and after taking another piercing look at the tremendous gulf, ran away in desperate excitement, seeking some other crossing. By the time he got back, baffled, of course, I had made a step or two. I dared not look back, but he made himself heard; and when he saw that I was certainly crossing, he cried aloud in despair. The danger was enough to daunt anybody, but it seems wonderful that he should have been able to weigh and appreciate it so justly. No mountaineer could have seen it more quickly or judged it more wisely, discriminating between real and apparent peril.

After I had gained the other side he howled louder than ever, and after running back and forth in vain search for a way of escape, he would return to the brink of the crevasse above the bridge, moaning and groaning as if in the bitterness of death. Could this be the silent, philosophic Stickeen? I shouted encouragement, telling him the bridge was not so bad as it looked, that I had left it flat for his feet, and he could walk it easily. But he was afraid to try it. Strange that so small an animal should be capable of such big, wise fears! I called again and again in a reassuring tone to come on and fear nothing; that he could come if he would only try. Then he would hush for a moment, look again at the bridge, and shout his unshakable conviction that he could never, never come that way; then lie back in despair, as if howling: "Oh-o-o, what a place! No-o-o; I can never go-o-o down there!" His natural composure and courage had vanished utterly in a tumultuous storm of fear. Had the danger been less, his distress would have seemed ridiculous. But in this gulf—a huge, yawning sepulcher big enough to hold everybody in the territory—lay the shadow of death, and his heartrending cries might well have called Heaven to his help. Perhaps they did. So hidden before, he was transparent now, and one could see the workings of his mind like the movements of a clock out of its case. His voice and gestures were perfectly human, and his hopes and fears unmistakable, while he seemed to understand every word of mine. I was troubled at the thought of leaving him. It seemed impossible to get him to venture.

To compel him to try by fear of being left, I started off as if leaving him to his fate, and disappeared back of a hummock; but this did no good, for he only lay down and cried. So after hiding a few minutes, I went back to the brink of the crevasse, and in a severe tone of voice shouted across to him that now I must certainly leave him—I could wait no longer; and that if he would not come, all I could promise was that I would return to seek him next day. I warned him that if he went back to the woods the wolves would kill him, and finished by urging him once more by words and gestures to come on.

He knew very well what I meant, and at last, with the courage of despair, hushed and breathless, he lay down on the brink in the hollow I had made for my knees, pressed his body against the ice to get the advantage of the friction, gazed into the first step, put his little feet together, and slid them slowly down into it, bunching all four in it, and almost standing on his head. Then, without lifting them, as well as I could see through the snow, he slowly worked them over the edge of the step, and down into the next and the next in succession in the same way, and gained the bridge. Then lifting his feet with the regularity and slowness of the vibrations of a seconds' pendulum, as if counting and measuring one, two, three, holding himself in dainty poise, and giving separate attention to each little step, he gained the foot of the cliff, at the top of which I was kneeling to give him a lift should he get within reach.

Here he halted in dead silence, and it was here I feared he might fail, for dogs are poor climbers. I had no cord. If I had had one, I would have dropped a noose over his head and hauled him up. But while I was thinking whether an available cord might be made out of clothing, he was looking keenly into the series of notched steps and finger-holds of the ice-ladder I had made, as if counting them and fixing the position of each one in his mind. Then suddenly up he came, with a nervy, springy rush, hooking his paws into the notches and steps so quickly that I could not see how it was done, and whizzed past my head, safe at last!

And now came a scene! "Well done, well done, little boy! Brave boy!" I cried, trying to catch and caress him; but he would not be caught. Never before or since have I seen anything like so passionate a revulsion from the depths of despair to uncontrollable, exultant, triumphant joy. He flashed and darted hither and thither as if fairly demented, screaming and shouting, swirling round and round in giddy loops and circles like a leaf in a whirlwind, lying down and rolling over and over, sidewise and heels over head, pouring forth a tumultuous flood of hysterical cries and sobs and gasping mutterings. And when I ran up to him to shake him, fearing he might die of joy, he flashed off two or three hundred yards, his feet in a mist of motion; then, turning suddenly, he came back in wild rushes, and launched himself at my face, almost knocking me down, all the time screeching and screaming and shouting as if saying, "Saved! saved! saved!" Then away again, dropping suddenly at times with his feet in the air, trembling, and fairly sobbing. Such passionate emotion was enough to kill him. Moses' stately song of triumph after escaping the Egyptians and the Red Sea was nothing to it. Who could have guessed the capacity of the dull, enduring little fellow for all that most stirs this mortal frame? Nobody could have helped crying with him.

But there is nothing like work for toning down either excessive fear or joy. So I ran ahead, calling him, in as gruff a voice as I could command, to come on and stop his nonsense, for we had far to go, and it would soon be dark. Neither of us feared another trial like this. Heaven would surely count one enough for a lifetime. The ice ahead was gashed by thousands of crevasses, but they were common ones. The joy of deliverance burned in us like fire, and we ran without fatigue, every muscle, with immense rebound, glorying in its strength. Stickeen flew across everything in his way, and not till dark did he settle into his normal fox-like, gliding trot.

At last the mountains crowned with spruce came in sight, looming faintly in the gloaming, and we soon felt the solid rock beneath our feet, and were safe. Then came weariness. We stumbled down along the lateral moraine in the dark, over rocks and tree-trunks, through the bushes and devil-club thickets and mossy logs and boulders of the woods where we had sheltered ourselves in the morning. Then out on the level mud-slope of the terminal moraine. Danger had vanished, and so had our strength. We reached camp about ten o'clock, and found a big fire and a big supper. A party of Hoona Indians had visited Mr. Young, bringing a gift of porpoise-meat and wild strawberries, and hunter Joe had brought in a wild goat. But we lay down, too tired to eat much, and soon fell into a troubled sleep. The man who said, "The harder the toil the sweeter the rest," never was profoundly tired. Stickeen kept springing up and muttering in his sleep, no doubt dreaming that he was still on the brink of the crevasse; and so did I—that night and many others, long afterward, when I was nervous and overtired.

Thereafter Stickeen was a changed dog. During the rest of the trip, instead of holding aloof, he would come to me at night, when all was quiet about the camp-fire, and rest his head on my knee, with a look of devotion, as if I were his god. And often, as he caught my eye, he seemed to be trying to say, "Wasn't that an awful time we had together on the glacier?"

None of his old friends know what finally became of him. When my work for the season was done I departed for California, and never saw the dear little fellow again. Mr. Young wrote me that in the summer of 1883 he was stolen by a tourist at Fort Wrangel, and taken away on a steamer. His fate is wrapped in mystery. If alive he is very old. Most likely he has left this world—crossed the last crevasse—and gone to another. But he will not be forgotten. Come what may, to me Stickeen is immortal.

12

THE RIVER OF DOUBT

BY THEODORE ROOSEVELT

Of all the men so casually labeled "larger than life," one who truly earned that distinction was Theodore Roosevelt. The twenty-sixth president of the United States was a man unlike any other at his level of influence and authority. He loved the strenuous outdoor life, as a rancher, hunter, naturalist, and explorer. In 1914, with his brother Kermit, Roosevelt ventured down Amazon tributaries such as the Rio da Dúvida (River of Doubt), which had never been mapped. Death was a possibility that waited around ever bend. Starvation, poisonous snake and insect bites, hostile natives, and dangerous waters were everyday threats. And the threats sometimes took their toll. The following excerpt is from his book, Through the Brazilian Wilderness.

On February 27, 1914, shortly after midday, we started down the River of Doubt into the unknown. We were quite uncertain whether after a week we should find ourselves in the Gy-Parana, or after six weeks in the Madeira, or after three months we knew not where. That was why the river was rightly christened the Dúvida.

We had been camped close to the river, where the trail that follows the telegraph line crosses it by a rough bridge. As our laden dugouts swung into the stream, Amilcar and Miller and all the others of the Gy-Parana party were on the banks and the bridge to wave farewell and wish us good-by and good luck. It was the height of the rainy season, and the swollen torrent was swift and brown. Our camp was at about 12 degrees 1 minute latitude south and 60 degrees 15 minutes longitude west of Greenwich. Our general course was to be northward toward the equator, by waterway through the vast forest.

We had seven canoes, all of them dugouts. One was small, one was cranky, and two were old, waterlogged, and leaky. The other three were good. The two old canoes were lashed together, and the cranky one was lashed to one of the others. Kermit with two paddlers went in the smallest of the good canoes; Colonel Rondon and Lyra with three other paddlers in the next largest; and the doctor, Cherrie, and I in the largest with three paddlers. The remaining eight *camaradas*—there were sixteen in all—were equally divided between our two pairs of lashed canoes. Although our personal baggage was cut down to the limit necessary for health and efficiency, yet on such a trip as ours, where scientific work has to be done and where food for twenty-two men for an unknown period of time has to be carried, it is impossible not to take a good deal of stuff; and the seven dugouts were too heavily laden.

The paddlers were a strapping set. They were expert rivermen and men of the forest, skilled veterans in wilderness work. They were lithe as panthers and brawny as bears. They swam like waterdogs. They were equally at home with pole and paddle, with axe and machete; and one was a good cook and others were good men around camp. They looked like pirates in the pictures of Howard Pyle or Maxfield Parrish; one or two of them were pirates, and one worse than a pirate; but most of them were hard-working, willing, and cheerful. They were white—or, rather, the olive of southern Europe—black, copper-colored, and of all intermediate shades. In my canoe Luiz the steersman, the headman, was a Matto Grosso Negro; Julio the bowsman was from Bahia and of pure Portuguese blood; and the third man, Antonio, was a Parecis Indian.

The actual surveying of the river was done by Colonel Rondon and Lyra, with Kermit as their assistant. Kermit went first in his little canoe with the sighting-rod, on which two disks, one red and one white, were placed a metre apart. He selected a place which commanded as long vistas as possible up-stream and down, and which therefore might be at the angle of a bend; landed; cut away the branches which obstructed the view; and set up the sighting-pole—incidentally encountering maribundi wasps and swarms of biting and stinging ants. Lyra, from his station up-stream, with his telemetre established the distance, while Colonel Rondon with the compass took the direction, and made the records. Then they moved on to the point Kermit had left, and Kermit established a new point within their sight. The first half-day's work was slow. The general course of the stream was a trifle east of north, but at short intervals it bent and curved literally toward every point of the compass. Kermit landed nearly a hundred times, and we made but nine and a third kilometres.

My canoe ran ahead of the surveying canoes. The height of the water made the going easy, for most of the snags and fallen trees were well beneath the surface. Now and then, however, the swift water hurried us toward ripples that marked ugly spikes of sunken timber, or toward uprooted trees that stretched almost across the stream. Then the muscles stood out on the backs and arms of the paddlers as stroke on stroke they urged us away from and past the obstacle. If the leaning or fallen trees were the thorny, slender-stemmed bor-itana palms, which love the wet, they were often, although plunged beneath the river, in full and vigorous growth, their stems curving upward, and their frond-crowned tops shaken by the rushing water. It was interesting work, for no outsider had ever gone down or up this river or seen the country through which we were passing. The lofty and matted forest rose like a green wall on either hand. The trees were stately and beautiful. The looped and twisted vines hung from them like great ropes. Masses of epiphytes grew both on the dead trees and the living; some had huge leaves like elephants' ears. Now and then fragrant scents were blown to us from flowers on the banks. There were not many birds, and for the most part the forest was silent; rarely we heard strange calls from the depths of the woods, or saw a cormorant or ibis.

My canoe ran only a couple of hours. Then we halted to wait for the others. After a couple of hours more, as the surveyors had not turned up, we landed and made camp at a spot where the bank rose sharply for a hundred yards to a level stretch of ground. Our canoes were moored to trees. The axemen cleared a space for the tents; they were pitched, the baggage was brought up, and fires were kindled. The woods were almost soundless. Through them ran old tapir trails, but there was no fresh sign. Before nightfall the surveyors arrived. There were a few piums and gnats, and a few mosquitoes after dark, but not enough to make us uncomfortable. The small stingless bees, of slightly aromatic odor, swarmed while daylight lasted and crawled over our faces and hands; they were such tame, harmless little things that when they tickled too much I always tried to brush them away without hurting them. But they became a great nuisance after a while. It had been raining at intervals, and the weather was overcast; but after the sun went down the sky cleared. The stars were brilliant overhead, and the new moon hung in the west. It was a pleasant night, the air almost cool, and we slept soundly.

Next morning the two surveying canoes left immediately after breakfast. An hour later the two pairs of lashed canoes pushed off. I kept our canoe to let Cherrie collect, for in the early hours we could hear a number of birds in the woods near by. The most interesting birds he shot were a cotinga, brilliant turquoise-blue with a magenta-purple throat, and a big woodpecker, black above and cinnamon below with an entirely red head and neck. It was almost noon before we started. We saw a few more birds; there were fresh tapir and paca tracks at one point where we landed; once we heard howler monkeys from the depth of the forest, and once we saw a big otter in midstream.

As we drifted and paddled down the swirling brown current, through the vivid rain-drenched green of the tropic forest, the trees leaned over the river from both banks. When those that had fallen in the river at some narrow point were very tall, or where it happened that two fell opposite each other, they formed barriers which the men in the leading canoes cleared with their axes. There were many palms, both the burity with its stiff fronds like enormous fans, and a handsome species of bacaba, with very long, gracefully curving fronds. In places the palms stood close together, towering and slender, their stems a stately colonnade, their fronds an arched fretwork against the sky. Butterflies of many hues fluttered over the river. The day was overcast, with showers of rain. When the sun broke through rifts in the clouds, his shafts turned the forest to gold.

In mid-afternoon we came to the mouth of a big and swift affluent entering from the right. It was undoubtedly the Bandeira, which we had crossed well toward its head, some ten days before, on our road to Bonofacio. The Nhambiquaras had then told Colonel Rondon that it flowed into the Dúvida. After its junction, with the added volume of water, the river widened without losing its depth. It was so high that it had overflowed and stood among the trees on the lower levels. Only the higher stretches were dry. On the sheer banks where we landed we had to push the canoes for yards or rods through the branches of the submerged trees, hacking and hewing. There were occasional bays and ox-bows from which the current had shifted. In these the coarse marsh grass grew tall.

This evening we made camp on a flat of dry ground, densely wooded, of course, directly on the edge of the river and five feet above it. It was fine to see the speed and sinewy ease with which the choppers cleared an open space for the tents. Next morning, when we bathed before sunrise, we dived into deep water right from the shore, and from the moored canoes. This second day we made sixteen and a half kilometres along the course of the river, and nine kilometres in a straight line almost due north.

The following day, March 1, there was much rain—sometimes showers, sometimes vertical sheets of water. Our course was somewhat west of north and we made twenty and a half kilometres. We passed signs of Indian habitation. There were abandoned palm-leaf shelters on both banks. On the left bank we came to two or three old Indian fields, grown up with coarse fern and studded with the burned skeletons of trees. At the mouth of a brook which entered from the right some sticks stood in the water, marking the site of an old fish-trap. At one point we found the tough vine hand-rail of an Indian bridge running right across the river, a couple of feet above it. Evidently the bridge had been built at low water. Three stout poles had been driven into the stream-bed in a line at right angles to the current. The bridge had consisted of poles fastened to these supports, leading between them and from the support at each end to the banks. The rope of tough vines had been stretched as a hand-rail, necessary with such precarious footing. The rise of the river had swept away the bridge, but the props and the rope hand-rail remained. In the afternoon, from the boat, Cherrie shot a large dark-gray monkey with a prehensile tail. It was very good eating.

We camped on a dry level space, but a few feet above, and close beside, the river—so that our swimming-bath was handy. The trees were cleared and camp was made with orderly hurry. One of the men almost stepped on a poisonous coral-snake, which would have been a serious thing, as his feet were bare. But I had on stout shoes, and the fangs of these serpents—unlike those of the pit-vipers—are too short to penetrate good leather. I promptly put my foot on him, and he bit my shoe with harmless venom. It has been said that the brilliant hues of the coral-snake when in its native haunts really confer on it a concealing coloration. In the dark and tangled woods, and to an only less extent in the ordinary varied landscape, anything motionless, especially if partially hidden, easily eludes the eye. But against the dark-brown mould of the forest floor on which we found this coral snake its bright and varied coloration was distinctly revealing; infinitely more so than the duller mottling of the jararaca and other dangerous snakes of the genus Lachesis. In the same place, however, we found a striking example of genuine protective or mimetic coloration and shape. A rather large insect larva—at least we judged it to be a larval form, but we were none of us entomologists—bore a resemblance to a partially curled dry leaf which was fairly startling. The tail exactly resembled the stem or continuation of the midrib of the dead leaf. The flattened body was curled up at the sides, and veined and colored precisely like the leaf. The head, colored like the leaf, projected in front.

We were still in the Brazilian highlands. The forest did not teem with life. It was generally rather silent; we did not hear such a chorus of birds and mammals as we had occasionally heard even on our overland journey, when more than once we had been awakened at dawn by the howling, screaming, yelping, and chattering of monkeys, toucans, macaws, parrots, and parakeets. There were, however, from time to time, queer sounds from the forest, and after nightfall different kinds of frogs and insects uttered strange cries and calls. In volume and frequency these seemed to increase until midnight. Then they died away and before dawn everything was silent.

At this camp the carregadores ants completely devoured the doctor's undershirt, and ate holes in his mosquito-net; and they also ate the strap of Lyra's gun-case. The little stingless bees, of many kinds, swarmed in such multitudes, and were so persevering, that we had to wear our head-nets when we wrote or skinned specimens. The following day was almost without rain. It was delightful to drift and paddle slowly down the beautiful tropical river. Until mid-afternoon the current was not very fast, and the broad, deep, placid stream bent and curved in every direction, although the general course was northwest. The country was flat, and more of the land was under than above water. Continually we found ourselves travelling between stretches of marshy forest where for miles the water stood or ran among the trees. Once we passed a hillock. We saw brilliantly colored parakeets and trogons. At last the slow current quickened. Faster it went, and faster, until it began to run like a mill-race, and we heard the roar of rapids ahead. We pulled to the right bank, moored the canoes, and while most of the men pitched camp two or three of them accompanied us to examine the rapids. We had made twenty kilometres.

We soon found that the rapids were a serious obstacle. There were many curls, and one or two regular falls, perhaps six feet high. It would have been impossible to run them, and they stretched for nearly a mile. The carry, however, which led through woods and over rocks in a nearly straight line, was somewhat shorter. It was not an easy portage over which to carry heavy loads and drag heavy dug-out canoes. At the point where the descent was steepest there were great naked flats of friable sandstone and conglomerate. Over parts of these, where there was a surface of fine sand, there was a growth of coarse grass. Other parts were bare and had been worn by the weather into fantastic shapes—one projection looked like an old-fash-ioned beaver hat upside down. In this place, where the naked flats of rock showed the projection of the ledge through which the river had cut its course, the torrent rushed down a deep, sheer-sided, and extremely narrow channel. At one point it was less than two yards across, and for quite a distance not more than five or six yards. Yet only a mile or two above the rapids the deep, placid river was at least a hundred yards wide. It seemed extraordinary, almost impossible, that so broad a river could in so short a space of time contract its dimensions to the width of the strangled channel through which it now poured its entire volume.

This has for long been a station where the Nhambiquaras at intervals built their ephemeral villages and tilled the soil with the rude and destructive cultivation of savages. There were several abandoned old fields, where the dense growth of rank fern hid the tangle of burnt and fallen logs. Nor had the Nhambiquaras been long absent. In one trail we found what gypsies would have called a "pateran," a couple of branches arranged crosswise, eight leaves to a branch; it had some special significance, belonging to that class of signals, each with some peculiar and often complicated meaning, which are commonly used by many wild peoples. The Indians had thrown a simple bridge, consisting of four long poles, without a hand-rail, across one of the narrowest parts of the rock gorge through which the river foamed in its rapid descent. This sub-tribe of Indians was called the Navaite; we named the rapids after them, Navaite Rapids. By observation Lyra found them to be (in close approximation to) latitude 11 degrees 44 minutes south and longitude 60 degrees 18 minutes west from Greenwich.

We spent March 3 and 4 and the morning of the 5th in portaging around the rapids. The first night we camped in the forest beside the spot where we had halted. Next morning we moved the baggage to the foot of the rapids, where we intended to launch the canoes, and pitched our tents on the open sandstone flat. It rained heavily. The little bees were in such swarms as to be a nuisance. Many small stinging bees were with them, which stung badly. We were bitten by huge horse-flies, the size of bumblebees. More serious annoyance was caused by the pium and boroshuda flies during the hours of daylight, and by the polvora, the sand-flies, after dark. There were a few mosquitoes. The boroshudas were the worst pests; they brought the blood at once, and left marks that lasted for weeks. I did my writing in head-net and gauntlets. Fortunately we had with us several bottles of "fly dope"—so named on the label—put up, with the rest of our medicine, by Doctor Alexander Lambert; he had tested it in the north woods and found it excellent. I had never before been forced to use such an ointment, and had been reluctant to take it with me; but now I was glad enough to have it, and we all of us found it exceedingly useful. I would never again go into mosquito or sand-fly country without it. The effect of an application wears off after half an hour or so, and under many conditions, as when one is perspiring freely, it is of no use; but there are times when minute mosquitoes and gnats get through head-nets and under mosquito-bars, and when the ointments occasionally renewed may permit one to get sleep or rest which would otherwise be impossible of attainment. The termites got into our tent on the sand-flat, ate holes in Cherrie's mosquito-net and poncho, and were starting to work at our duffel-bags, when we discovered them.

Packing the loads across was simple. Dragging the heavy dugouts was labor. The biggest of the two water-logged ones was the heaviest. Lyra and Kermit did the job. All the men were employed at it except the cook, and one man who was down with fever. A road was chopped through the forest and a couple of hundred stout six-foot poles, or small logs, were cut as rollers and placed about two yards apart. With block and tackle the seven dugouts were hoisted out of the river up the steep banks, and up the rise of ground until the level was reached. Then the men harnessed themselves two by two on the drag-rope, while one of their number pried behind with a lever, and the canoe, bumping and sliding, was twitched through the woods. Over the sandstone flats there were some ugly ledges, but on the whole the course was down-hill and relatively easy. Looking at the way the work was done, at the good-will, the endurance, and the bull-like strength of the *camaradas*, and at the intelligence and the unwearied efforts of their commanders, one could but wonder at the ignorance of those who do not realize the energy and the power that are so often possessed by, and that may be so readily developed in, the men of the tropics.

Another subject of perpetual wonder is the attitude of certain men who stay at home, and still more the attitude of certain men who travel under easy conditions, and who belittle the achievements of the real explorers of, the real adventures in, the great wilderness. The impostors and romancers among explorers or would-be explorers and wilderness wanderers have been unusually prominent in connection with South America (although the conspicuous ones are not South Americans, by the way); and these are fit subjects for condemnation and derision. But the work of the genuine explorer and wilderness wanderer is fraught with fatigue, hardship, and danger. Many of the men of little knowledge talk glibly of portaging as if it were simple and easy. A portage over rough and unknown ground is always a work of difficulty and of some risk to the canoe; and in the untrodden, or even in the unfrequented, wilderness, risk to the canoe is a serious matter. This particular portage at Navaite Rapids was far from being unusually difficult; yet it not only cost two and a half days of severe and incessant labor, but it cost something in damage to the canoes. One in particular, the one in which I had been journeying, was split in a manner which caused us serious uneasiness as to how long, even after being patched, it would last. Where the canoes were launched, the bank was sheer, and one of the water-logged canoes filled and went to the bottom; and there was more work in raising it.

We were still wholly unable to tell where we were going or what lay ahead of us. Round the camp-fire, after supper, we held endless discussions and hazarded all kinds of guesses on both subjects. The river might bend sharply to the west and enter the Gy-Parana high up or low down, or go north to the Madeira, or bend eastward and enter the Tapajos, or fall into the Canuma and finally through one of its mouths enter the Amazon direct. Lyra inclined to the first, and Colonel Rondon to the second, of these propositions. We did not know whether we had one hundred or eight hundred kilometres to go, whether the stream would be fairly smooth or whether we would encounter waterfalls, or rapids, or even some big marsh or lake. We could not tell whether or not we would meet hostile Indians, although no one of us ever went ten yards from camp without his rifle. We had no idea how much time the trip would take. We had entered a land of unknown possibilities.

We started down-stream again early in the afternoon of March 5. Our hands and faces were swollen from the bites and stings of the insect pests at the sand-flat camp, and it was a pleasure once more to be in the middle of the river, where they did not come, in any numbers, while we were in motion. The current was swift, but the river was so deep that there were no serious obstructions. Twice we went down over slight riffles, which in the dry season were doubtless rapids; and once we struck a spot where many whirlpools marked the presence underneath of boulders which would have been above water had not the river been so swollen by the rains. The distance we covered in a day going down-stream would have taken us a week if we had been going up. The course wound hither and thither, sometimes in sigmoid curves; but the general direction was east of north.

As usual, it was very beautiful; and we never could tell what might appear around any curve. In the forest that rose on either hand were tall rubber-trees. The surveying canoes, as usual, went first, while I shepherded the two pairs of lashed cargo canoes. I kept them always between me and the surveying canoes—ahead of me until I passed the surveying canoes, then behind me until, after an hour or so, I had chosen a place to camp. There was so much overflowed ground that it took us some little time this afternoon before we found a flat place high enough to be dry. Just before reaching camp Cherrie shot a jacu, a handsome bird somewhat akin to, but much smaller than, a turkey; after Cherrie had taken its skin, its body made an excellent canja. We saw parties of monkeys; and the false bellbirds uttered their ringing whistles in the dense timber around our tents. The giant ants, an inch and a quarter long, were rather too plentiful around this camp; one stung Kermit; it was almost like the sting of a small scorpion, and pained severely for a couple of hours. This half-day we made twelve kilometres.

On the following day we made nineteen kilometres, the river twisting in every direction, but in its general course running a little west of north. Once we stopped at a bee-tree, to get honey. The tree was a towering giant, of the kind called milk-tree, because a thick milky juice runs freely from any cut. Our *camaradas* eagerly drank the white fluid that flowed from the wounds made by their axes. I tried it. The taste was not unpleasant, but it left a sticky feeling in the mouth. The helmsman of my boat, Luiz, a powerful Negro, chopped into the tree, balancing himself with springy ease on a slight scaffolding. The honey was in a hollow, and had been made by medium-sized stingless bees. At the mouth of the hollow they had built a curious entrance of their own, in the shape of a spout of wax about a foot long. At the opening the walls of the spout showed the wax formation, but elsewhere it had become in color and texture indistinguishable from the bark of the tree. The honey was delicious, sweet and yet with a tart flavor. The comb differed much from that of our honey-bees. The honey-cells were very large, and the brood-cells, which were small, were in a single instead of a double row.

By this tree I came across an example of genuine concealing coloration. A huge tree-toad, the size of a bullfrog, was seated upright—not squatted flat—on a big rotten limb. It was absolutely motionless; the yellow brown of its back, and its dark sides, exactly harmonized in color with the light and dark patches on the log; the color was as concealing, here in its natural surroundings, as is the color of our common wood-frog among the dead leaves of our woods. When I stirred it up it jumped to a small twig, catching hold with the disks of its finger-tips, and balancing itself with unexpected ease for so big a creature, and then hopped to the ground and again stood motionless. Evidently it trusted for safety to escaping observation. We saw some monkeys and fresh tapir sign, and Kermit shot a jacu for the pot.

At about three o'clock I was in the lead, when the current began to run more quickly. We passed over one or two decided ripples, and then heard the roar of rapids ahead, while the stream began to race. We drove the canoe into the bank, and then went down a tapir trail, which led alongside the river, to reconnoiter. A quarter of a mile's walk showed us that there were big rapids, down which the canoes could not go; and we returned to the landing. All the canoes had gathered there, and Rondon, Lyra, and Kermit started down-stream to explore. They returned in an hour, with the information that the rapids continued for a long distance, with falls and steep pitches of broken water, and that the portage would take several days. We made camp just above the rapids. Ants swarmed, and some of them bit savagely. Our men, in clearing away the forest for our tents, left several very tall and slender accashy palms; the bole of this palm is as straight as an arrow and is crowned with delicate, gracefully curved fronds. We had come along the course of the river almost exactly a hundred kilometres; it had twisted so that we were only about fifty-five kilometres north of our starting-point. The rock was porphyritic.

The 7th, 8th, and 9th we spent in carrying the loads and dragging and floating the dugouts past the series of rapids at whose head we had stopped.

The first day we shifted camp a kilometre and a half to the foot of this series of rapids. This was a charming and picturesque camp. It was at the edge of the river, where there was a little, shallow bay with a beach of firm sand. In the water, at the middle point of the beach, stood a group of three burity palms, their great trunks rising like columns. Round the clearing in which our tents stood were several very big trees; two of them were rubber-trees. Kermit went down-stream five or six kilometres, and returned, having shot a jacu and found that at the point which he had reached there was another rapids, almost a fall, which would necessitate our again dragging the canoes over a portage. Antonio, the Parecis, shot a big monkey; of this I was glad because portaging is hard work, and the men appreciated the meat. So far Cherrie had collected sixty birds on the Dúvida, all of them new to the collection, and some probably new to science. We saw the fresh sign of paca, agouti, and the small peccary, and Kermit with the dogs roused a tapir, which crossed the river right through the rapids; but no one got a shot at it.

Except at one or perhaps two points a very big dugout, lightly loaded, could probably run all these rapids. But even in such a canoe it would be silly to make the attempt on an exploring expedition, where the loss of a canoe or of its contents means disaster; and moreover such a canoe could not be taken, for it would be impossible to drag it over the portages on the occasions when the portages became inevitable. Our canoes would not have lived half a minute in the wild water.

On the second day the canoes and loads were brought down to the foot of the first rapids. Lyra cleared the path and laid the logs for rollers, while Kermit dragged the dugouts up the bank from the water with block and tackle, with strain of rope and muscle. Then they joined forces, as over the uneven ground it needed the united strength of all their men to get the heavy dugouts along. Meanwhile the colonel with one attendant measured the distance, and then went on a long hunt, but saw no game. I strolled down beside the river for a couple of miles, but also saw nothing. In the dense tropical forest of the Amazonian basin hunting is very difficult, especially for men who are trying to pass through the country as rapidly as possible. On such a trip as ours getting game is largely a matter of chance.

On the following day Lyra and Kermit brought down the canoes and loads, with hard labor, to the little beach by the three palms where our tents were pitched. Many pacovas [wild bananas] grew round about. The men used their immense leaves, some of which were twelve feet long and two and a half feet broad, to roof the flimsy shelters under which they hung their hammocks. I went into the woods, but in the tangle of vegetation it would have been a mere hazard had I seen any big animal. Generally the woods were silent and empty. Now and then little troops of birds of many kinds passed—woodhewers, ant-thrushes, tanagers, flycatchers; as in the spring and fall similar troops of warblers, chickadees, and nuthatches pass through our northern woods. On the rocks and on the great trees by the river grew beautiful white and lilac orchids, the sobralia, of sweet and delicate fragrance. For the moment my own books seemed a trifle heavy, and perhaps I would have found the day tedious if Kermit had not lent me the *Oxford Book of French Verse*. Eustache Deschamp, Joachim du

Bellay, Ronsard, the delightful La Fontaine, the delightful but appalling Villon, Victor Hugo's "Guitare," Madame Desbordes-Valmore's lines on the little girl and her pillow, as dear little verses about a child as ever were written—these and many others comforted me much, as I read them in head-net and gauntlets, sitting on a log by an unknown river in the Amazonian forest.

On the 10th we again embarked and made a kilometre and a half, spending most of the time in getting past two more rapids. Near the first of these we saw a small cayman, a jacare-tinga. At each set of rapids the canoes were unloaded and the loads borne past on the shoulders of the *camaradas*; three of the canoes were paddled down by a couple of naked paddlers apiece; and the two sets of double canoes were let down by ropes, one of one couple being swamped but rescued and brought safely to shore on each occasion. One of the men was upset while working in the swift water, and his face was cut against the stones. Lyra and Kermit did the actual work with the *camaradas*. Kermit, dressed substantially like the *camaradas* themselves, worked in the water, and, as the overhanging branches were thronged with crowds of biting and stinging ants, he was marked and blistered over his whole body. Indeed, we all suffered more or less from these ants, while the swarms of biting flies grew constantly more numerous. The termites ate holes in my helmet and also in the cover of my cot. Every one else had a hammock. At this camp we had come down the river about 102 kilometres, according to the surveying records, and in height had descended nearly 100 metres, as shown by the aneroid—although the figure in this case is only an approximation, as an aneroid cannot be depended on for absolute accuracy of results.

Next morning we found that during the night we had met with a serious misfortune. We had halted at the foot of the rapids. The canoes were moored to trees on the bank, at the tail of the broken water. The two old canoes, although one of them was our biggest cargo-carrier, were water-logged and heavy, and one of them was leaking. In the night the river rose. The leaky canoe, which at best was too low in the water, must have gradually filled from the wash of the waves. It sank, dragging down the other; they began to roll, bursting their moorings; and in the morning they had disappeared. A canoe was launched to look for them; but, rolling over the boulders on the rocky bottom, they had at once been riven asunder, and the big fragments that were soon found, floating in eddies, or along the shore, showed that it was useless to look farther. We called these rapids Broken Canoe Rapids.

It was not pleasant to have to stop for some days; thanks to the rapids, we had made slow progress, and with our necessarily limited supply of food, and no knowledge whatever of what was ahead of us, it was important to make good time. But there was no alternative. We had to build either one big canoe or two small ones. It was raining heavily as the men started to explore in different directions for good canoe trees. Three—which ultimately proved not very good for the purpose—were found close to camp; splendid-looking trees, one of them five feet in diameter three feet from the ground. The axemen immediately attacked this one under the superintendence of Colonel Rondon. Lyra and Kermit started in opposite directions to hunt. Lyra killed a jacu for us, and Kermit killed two monkeys for the men. Toward night fall it cleared. The moon was nearly full, and the foaming river gleamed like silver.

Our men were "regional volunteers," that is, they had enlisted in the service of the Telegraphic Commission especially to do this wilderness work, and were highly paid, as was fitting, in view of the toil, hardship, and hazard to life and health. Two of them had been with Colonel Rondon during his eight months' exploration in 1909, at which time his men were regulars, from his own battalion of engineers. His four aides during the closing months of this trip were Lieutenants Lyra, Amarante, Alencarliense, and Pyrineus. The naturalist Miranda Ribeiro also accompanied him. This was the year when, marching on foot through an absolutely unknown wilderness, the colonel and his party finally reached the Gy-Parana, which on the maps was then (and on most maps is now) placed in an utterly wrong course, and over a degree out of its real position. When they reached the affluents of the Gy-Parana a third of the members of the party were so weak with fever that they could hardly crawl. They had no baggage. Their clothes were in tatters, and some of the men were almost naked. For months they had had no food except what little game they shot, and especially the wild fruits and nuts; if it had not been for the great abundance of the Brazil-nuts they would all have died.

At the first big stream they encountered they built a canoe, and Alencarliense took command of it and descended to map the course of the river. With him went Ribeiro, the doctor Tanageira, who could no longer walk on account of the ulceration of one foot, three men whom the fever had rendered unable longer to walk, and six men who were as yet well enough to handle the canoe. By the time the remainder of the party came to the next navigable river eleven more fever-stricken men had nearly reached the end of their tether. Here they ran across a poor devil who had for four months been lost in the forest and was dying of slow starvation. He had eaten nothing but Brazil-nuts and the grubs of insects. He could no longer walk, but could sit erect and totter feebly for a few feet.

Another canoe was built, and in it Pyrineus started down-stream with the eleven fever patients and the starving wanderer. Colonel Rondon kept up the morale of his men by still carrying out the forms of military discipline. The ragged bugler had his bugle. Lieutenant Pyrineus had lost every particle of his clothing except a hat and a pair of drawers. The half-naked lieutenant drew up his eleven fever patients in line; the bugle sounded; every one came to attention; and the haggard colonel read out the orders of the day. Then the dugout with its load of sick men started down-stream, and Rondon, Lyra, Amarante, and the twelve remaining men resumed their weary march. When a fortnight later they finally struck a camp of rubber-gatherers three of the men were literally and entirely naked. Meanwhile Amilcar had ascended the Jacyparana a month or two previously with provisions to meet them; for at that time the maps incorrectly treated this river as larger, instead of smaller, than the Gy-Parana, which they were in fact descending; and Colonel Rondon had supposed that they were going down the former stream. Amilcar returned after himself suffering much hardship and danger. The different parties finally met at the mouth of the Gy-Parana, where it enters the Madeira. The lost man whom they had found seemed on the road to recovery, and they left him at a ranch, on the Madeira, where he could be cared for; yet after they had left him they heard that he had died.

On the 12th the men were still hard at work hollowing out the hard wood of the big tree, with axe and adze, while watch and ward were kept over them to see that the idlers did not shirk at the expense of the industrious. Kermit and Lyra again hunted; the former shot a curassow, which was welcome, as we were endeavoring in all ways to economize our food supply. We were using the tops of palms also. I spent the day hunting in the woods, for the most part by the river, but saw nothing. In the season of the rains game is away from the river and fish are scarce and turtles absent. Yet it was pleasant to be in the great silent forest. Here and there grew immense trees, and on some of them mighty buttresses sprang from the base. The lianas and vines were of every size and shape. Some were twisted and some were not. Some came down straight and slender from branches a hundred feet above. Others curved like long serpents around the trunks. Others were like knotted cables. In the shadow there was little noise. The wind rarely moved the hot, humid air. There were few flowers or birds. Insects were altogether too abundant, and even when travelling slowly it was impossible always to avoid them—not to speak of our constant companions the bees, mosquitoes, and especially the boroshudas or bloodsucking flies.

Now while bursting through a tangle I disturbed a nest of wasps, whose resentment was active; now I heedlessly stepped among the outliers of a small party of the carnivorous foraging ants; now, grasping a branch as I stumbled, I shook down a shower of fire ants; and among all these my attention was particularly arrested by the bite of one of the giant ants, which stung like a hornet, so that I felt it for three hours. The *camaradas* generally went barefoot or only wore sandals; and their ankles and feet were swollen and inflamed from the bites of the boroshudas and ants, some being actually incapacitated from work. All of us suffered more or less, our faces and hands swelling slightly from the boroshuda bites; and in spite of our clothes we were bitten all over our bodies, chiefly by ants and the small forest ticks. Because of the rain and the heat our clothes were usually wet when we took them off at night, and just as wet when we put them on again in the morning.

All day on the 13th the men worked at the canoe, making good progress. In rolling and shifting the huge, heavy tree-trunk every one had to assist now and then. The work continued until ten in the evening, as the weather was clear. After nightfall some of the men held candles and the others plied axe or adze, standing within or beside the great, half-hollowed logs, while the flicker of the lights showed the tropic forest rising in the darkness round about. The night air was hot and still and heavy with moisture. The men were stripped to the waist. Olive and copper and ebony, their skins glistened as if oiled, and rippled with the ceaseless play of the thews beneath.

On the morning of the 14th the work was resumed in a torrential tropic downpour. The canoe was finished, dragged down to the water, and launched soon after midday, and another hour or so saw us under way. The descent was marked, and the swollen river raced along. Several times we passed great whirlpools, sometimes shifting, sometimes steady. Half a dozen times we ran over rapids, and, although they were not high enough to have been obstacles to loaded Canadian canoes, two of them were serious to us. Our heavily laden, clumsy dugouts were sunk to within three or four inches of the surface of the river, and, although they were buoyed on each side with bundles of burity-palm branch-stems, they shipped a great deal of water in the rapids. The two biggest rapids we only just made, and after each we had hastily to push ashore in order to bail. In one set of big ripples or waves my canoe was nearly swamped. In a wilderness, where what is ahead is absolutely unknown, alike in terms of time, space, and method—for we had no idea where we would come out, how we would get out, or when we would get out—it is of vital consequence not to lose one's outfit, especially the provisions; and yet it is of only less consequence to go as rapidly as possible lest all the provisions be exhausted and the final stages of the expedition be accomplished by men weakened from semi-starvation, and therefore ripe for disaster. On this occasion, of the two hazards, we felt it necessary to risk running the rapids; for our progress had been so very slow that unless we made up the time, it was probable that we would be short of food before we got where we could expect to procure any more except what little the country, in the time of the rains and floods, might yield. We ran until after five, so that the work of pitching camp was finished in the dark. We had made nearly sixteen kilometres in a direction slightly east of north. This evening the air was fresh and cool.

The following morning, the 15th of March, we started in good season. For six kilometres we drifted and paddled down the swift river without incident. At times we saw lofty Brazil-nut trees rising above the rest of the forest on the banks; and back from the river these trees grow to enormous proportions, towering like giants. There were great rubber-trees also, their leaves always in sets of threes. Then the ground on either hand rose into boulder-strewn, forest-clad hills and the roar of broken water announced that once more our course was checked by dangerous rapids. Round a bend we came on them; a wide descent of white water, with an island in the middle, at the upper edge. Here grave misfortune befell us, and graver misfortune was narrowly escaped.

Kermit, as usual, was leading in his canoe. It was the smallest and least seaworthy of all. He had in it little except a week's supply of our boxed provisions and a few tools; fortunately none of the food for the *camaradas*. His dog Trigueiro was with him. Besides himself, the crew consisted of two men: Joao, the helmsman, or pilot, as he is called in Brazil, and Simplicio, the bowsman. Both were Negroes and exceptionally good men in every way. Kermit halted his canoe on the left bank, above the rapids, and waited for the colonel's canoe. Then the colonel and Lyra walked down the bank to see what was ahead. Kermit took his canoe across to the island to see whether the descent could be better accomplished on the other side. Having made his investigation, he ordered the men to return to the bank he had left, and the dugout was headed up-stream accordingly.

Before they had gone a dozen yards, the paddlers digging their paddles with all their strength into the swift current, one of the shifting whirlpools of which I have spoken came down-stream, whirled them around, and swept them so close to the rapids that no human power could avoid going over them. As they were drifting into them broadside on, Kermit yelled to the steersman to turn her head, so as to take them in the only way that offered any chance whatever of safety. The water came aboard, wave after wave, as they raced down. They reached the bottom with the canoe upright, but so full as barely to float, and the paddlers urged her toward the shore. They had nearly reached the bank when another whirlpool or whirling eddy tore them away and hurried them back to midstream, where the dugout filled and turned over.

Joao, seizing the rope, started to swim ashore; the rope was pulled from his hand, but he reached the bank. Poor Simplicio must have been pulled under at once and his life beaten out on the boulders beneath the racing torrent. He never rose again, nor did we ever recover his body. Kermit clutched his rifle, his favorite .405 Winchester with which he had done most of his hunting both in Africa and America, and climbed on the bottom of the upset boat. In a minute he was swept into the second series of rapids, and whirled away from the rolling boat, losing his rifle. The water beat his helmet down over his head and face and drove him beneath the surface; and when he rose at last he was almost drowned, his breath and strength almost spent. He was in swift but quiet water, and swam toward an overhanging branch. His jacket hindered him, but he knew he was too nearly gone to be able to get it off, and, thinking with the curious calm one feels when death is but a moment away, he realized that the utmost his failing strength could do was to reach the branch. He reached, and clutched it, and then almost lacked strength to haul himself out on the land. Good Trigueiro had faithfully swum alongside him through the rapids, and now himself scrambled ashore. It was a very narrow escape. Kermit was a great comfort and help to me on the trip; but the fear of some fatal accident befalling him was always a nightmare to me. He was to be married as soon as the trip was over; and it did not seem to me that I could bear to bring bad tidings to his betrothed and to his mother.

Simplicio was unmarried. Later we sent to his mother all the money that would have been his had he lived. The following morning we put on one side of the post erected to mark our camping-spot the following inscription, in Portuguese: IN THESE RAPIDS DIED POOR SIMPLICIO.

On an expedition such as ours death is one of the accidents that may at any time occur, and narrow escapes from death are too common to be felt as they would be felt elsewhere. One mourns sincerely, but mourning cannot interfere with labor. We immediately proceeded with the work of the portage. From the head to the tail of this series of rapids the distance was about six hundred yards. A path was cut along the bank, over which the loads were brought. The empty canoes ran the rapids without mishap, each with two skilled paddlers. One of the canoes almost ran into a swimming tapir at the head of the rapids; it went down the rapids, and then climbed out of the river. Kermit, accompanied by Joao, went three or four miles down the river, looking for the body of Simplicio and for the sunk canoe. He found neither. But he found a box of provisions and a paddle, and salvaged both by swimming into midstream after them. He also found that a couple of kilometres below there was another stretch of rapids, and following them on the left-hand bank to the foot he found that they were worse than the ones we had just passed, and impassable for canoes on this left-hand side.

We camped at the foot of the rapids we had just passed. There were many small birds here, but it was extremely difficult to see or shoot them in the lofty tree tops, and to find them in the tangle beneath if they were shot. However, Cherrie got four species new to the collection. One was a tiny hummer, one of the species known as woodstars, with dainty but not brilliant plumage; its kind is never found except in the deep, dark woods, not coming out into the sunshine. Its crop was filled with ants; when shot it was feeding at a cluster of long red flowers. He also got a very handsome trogon and an exquisite little tanager, as brilliant as a cluster of jewels; its throat was lilac, its breast turquoise, its crown and forehead topaz, while above it was glossy purple-black, the lower part of the back ruby-red. This tanager was a female; I can hardly imagine that the male is more brilliantly colored. The fourth bird was a queer hawk of the genus Ibycter, black, with a white belly, naked red cheeks and throat and red legs and feet. Its crop was filled with the seeds of fruits and a few insect remains; an extraordinary diet for a hawk.

The morning of the 16th was dark and gloomy. Through sheets of blinding rain we left our camp of misfortune for another camp where misfortune also awaited us. Less than half an hour took our dugouts to the head of the rapids below. As Kermit had already explored the left-hand side, Colonel Rondon and Lyra went down the right-hand side and found a channel which led round the worst part, so that they deemed it possible to let down the canoes by ropes from the bank. The distance to the foot of the rapids was about a kilometre. While the loads were being brought down the left bank, Luiz and Antonio Correa, our two best watermen, started to take a canoe down the right side, and Colonel Rondon walked ahead to see anything he could about the river. He was accompanied by one of our three dogs, Lobo.

After walking about a kilometre he heard ahead a kind of howling noise, which he thought was made by spider-monkeys. He walked in the direction of the sound and Lobo ran ahead. In a minute he heard Lobo yell with pain, and then, still yelping, come toward him, while the creature that was howling also approached, evidently in pursuit. In a moment a second yell from Lobo, followed by silence, announced that he was dead; and the sound of the howling when near convinced Rondon that the dog had been killed by an Indian, doubtless with two arrows. Probably the Indian was howling to lure the spider-monkeys toward him. Rondon fired his rifle in the air, to warn off the Indian or Indians, who in all probability had never seen an outsider, and certainly could not imagine that one was in the neighborhood.

He then returned to the foot of the rapids, where the portage was still going on, and, in company with Lyra, Kermit, and Antonio Parecis, the Indian, walked back to where Lobo's body lay. Sure enough he found him, slain by two arrows. One arrow-head was in him, and nearby was a strange stick used in the very primitive method of fishing of all these Indians. Antonio recognized its purpose. The Indians, who were apparently two or three in number, had fled. Some beads and trinkets were left on the spot to show that we were not angry and were friendly.

Meanwhile Cherrie stayed at the head and I at the foot of the portage as guards. Luiz and Antonio Correa brought down one canoe safely. The next was the new canoe, which was very large and heavy, being made of wood that would not float. In the rapids the rope broke, and the canoe was lost, Luiz being nearly drowned.

It was a very bad thing to lose the canoe, but it was even worse to lose the rope and pulleys. This meant that it would be physically impossible to hoist big canoes up even small hills or rocky hillocks, such as had been so frequent beside the many rapids we had encountered. It was not wise to spend the four days necessary to build new canoes where we were, in danger of attack from the Indians. Moreover, new rapids might be very near, in which case the new canoes would hamper us. Yet the four remaining canoes would not carry all the loads and all the men, no matter how we cut the loads down; and we intended to cut everything down at once.

We had been gone eighteen days. We had used over a third of our food. We had gone only 125 kilometres, and it was probable that we had at least five times, perhaps six or seven times, this distance still to go. We had taken a fortnight to descend rapids amounting in the aggregate to less than seventy yards of fall; a very few yards of fall makes a dangerous rapid when the river is swollen and swift and there are obstructions. We had only one aneroid to determine our altitude, and therefore could make merely a loose approximation to it, but we probably had between two and three times this descent in the aggregate of rapids ahead of us. So far the country had offered little in the way of food except palm-tops. We had lost four canoes and one man. We were in the country of wild Indians, who shot well with their bows. It behooved us to go warily, but also to make all speed possible, if we were to avoid serious trouble.

The best plan seemed to be to march thirteen men down along the bank, while the remaining canoes, lashed two and two, floated down beside them. If after two or three days we found no bad rapids, and there seemed a reasonable chance of going some distance at decent speed, we could then build the new canoes—preferably two small ones, this time, instead of one big one. We left all the baggage we could. We were already down as far as comfort would permit; but we now struck off much of the comfort. Cherrie, Kermit, and I had been sleeping under a very light fly; and there was another small light tent for one person, kept for possible emergencies. The last was given to me for my cot, and all five of the others swung their hammocks under the big fly. This meant that we left two big and heavy tents behind. A box of surveying instruments was also abandoned. Each of us got his personal belongings down to one box or duffel-bag—although there was only a small diminution thus made; because we had so little that the only way to make a serious diminution was to restrict ourselves to the clothes on our backs.

The biting flies and ants were to us a source of discomfort and at times of what could fairly be called torment. But to the *camaradas*, most of whom went barefoot or only wore sandals—and they never did or would wear shoes—the effect was more serious. They wrapped their legs and feet in pieces of canvas or hide; and the feet of three of them became so swollen that they were crippled and could not walk any distance. The doctor, whose courage and cheerfulness never flagged, took excellent care of them. Thanks to him, there had been among them hitherto but one or two slight cases of fever. He administered to each man daily a half-gram—nearly eight grains—of quinine, and every third or fourth day a double dose.

The following morning Colonel Rondon, Lyra, Kermit, Cherrie, and nine of the *camaradas* started in single file down the bank, while the doctor and I went in the two double canoes, with six *camaradas*, three of them the invalids with swollen feet. We halted continually, as we went about three times as fast as the walkers; and we traced the course of the river. After forty minutes' actual going in the boats we came to some rapids; the unloaded canoes ran them without difficulty, while the loads were portaged. In an hour and a half we were again under way, but in ten minutes came to other rapids, where the river ran among islands, and there were several big curls. The clumsy, heavily laden dugouts, lashed in couples, were unwieldy and hard to handle. The rapids came just round a sharp bend, and we got caught in the upper part of the swift water and had to run the first set of rapids in consequence. We in the leading pair of dugouts were within an ace of coming to grief on some big boulders against which we were swept by a cross current at the turn. All of us paddling hard—scraping and bumping—we got through by the skin of our teeth, and managed to make the bank and moor our dugouts. It was a narrow escape from grave disaster. The second pair of lashed dugouts profited by our experience, and made the run—with risk, but with less risk—and moored beside us. Then all the loads were taken out, and the empty canoes were run down through the least dangerous channels among the islands.

This was a long portage, and we camped at the foot of the rapids, having made nearly seven kilometres. Here a little river, a rapid stream of volume equal to the Dúvida at the point where we first embarked, joined from the west. Colonel Rondon and Kermit came to it first, and the former named it Rio Kermit. There was in it a waterfall about six or eight feet high, just above the junction. Here we found plenty of fish. Lyra caught two pacu, good-sized, deep-bodied fish. They were delicious eating. Antonio the Parecis said that these fish never came up heavy rapids in which there were falls they had to jump. We could only hope that he was correct, as in that case the rapids we would encounter in the future would rarely be so serious as to necessitate our dragging the heavy dugouts overland. Passing the rapids we had hitherto encountered had meant severe labor and some danger. But the event showed that he was mistaken. The worst rapids were ahead of us.

While our course as a whole had been almost due north, and sometimes east of north, yet where there were rapids the river had generally, although not always, turned westward. This seemed to indicate that to the east of us there was a low northward projection of the central plateau across which we had travelled on mule-back. This is the kind of projection that appears on the maps of this region as a sierra. Probably it sent low spurs to the west, and the farthest points of these spurs now and then caused rapids in our course (for the rapids generally came where there were hills) and for the moment deflected the river westward from its general downhill trend to the north.

There was no longer any question that the Dúvida was a big river, a river of real importance. It was not a minor affluent of some other affluent. But we were still wholly in the dark as to where it came out. It was still possible, although exceedingly improbable, that it entered the Gy-Parana, as another river of substantially the same size, near its mouth. It was much more likely, but not probable, that it entered the Tapajos. It was probable, although far from certain, that it entered the Madeira low down, near its point of junction with the Amazon. In this event it was likely, although again far from certain, that its mouth would prove to be the Aripuanan. The Aripuanan does not appear on the maps as a river of any size; on a good standard map of South America which I had with me its name does not appear at all, although a dotted indication of a small river or creek at about the right place probably represents it. Nevertheless, from the report of one of his lieutenants who had examined its mouth, and from the stories of the rubber-gatherers, or *seringueiros*, Colonel Rondon had come to the conclusion that this was the largest affluent of the Madeira, with such a body of water that it must have a big drainage basin. He thought that the Dúvida was probably one of its head streams—although every existing map represented the lay of the land to be such as to render impossible the existence of such a river system and drainage basin. The rubber-gatherers reported that they had gone many days' journey up the river, to a point where there was a series of heavy rapids with above them the junction point of two large rivers, one entering from the west. Beyond this they had difficulties because of the hostility of the Indians; and where the junction point was no one could say. On the chance Colonel Rondon had directed one of his subordinate officers, Lieutenant Pyrineus, to try to meet us, with boats and provisions, by ascending the Aripuanan to the point of entry of its first big affluent. This was the course followed when Amilcar had been directed to try to meet the explorers who in 1909 came down the Gy-Parana. At that time the effort was a failure, and the two parties never met; but we might have better luck, and in any event the chance was worth taking.

On the morning following our camping by the mouth of the Rio Kermit, Colonel Rondon took a good deal of pains in getting a big post set up at the entry of the smaller river into the Dúvida. Then he summoned me, and all the others, to attend the ceremony of its erection. We found the *camaradas* drawn up in line, and the colonel preparing to read aloud "the orders of the day." To the post was nailed a board with "Rio Kermit" on it; and the colonel read the orders, reciting that by the direction of the Brazilian Government, and inasmuch as the unknown river was evidently a great river, he formally christened it the Rio Roosevelt.

This was a complete surprise to me. Both Lauro Miller and Colonel Rondon had spoken to me on the subject, and I had urged, and Kermit had urged, as strongly as possible, that the name be kept as Rio da Dúvida. We felt that the "River of Doubt" was an unusually good name; and it is always well to keep a name of this character. But my kind friends insisted otherwise, and it would have been churlish of me to object longer. I was much touched by their action, and by the ceremony itself. At the conclusion of the reading Colonel Rondon led in cheers for the United States and then for me and for Kermit; and the *camaradas* cheered with a will. I proposed three cheers for Brazil and then for Colonel Rondon, and Lyra, and the doctor, and then for all the *camaradas*. Then Lyra said that everybody had been cheered except Cherrie; and so we all gave three cheers for Cherrie, and the meeting broke up in high good humor.

Immediately afterward the walkers set off on their march downstream, looking for good canoe trees. In a quarter of an hour we followed with the canoes. As often as we overtook them we halted until they had again gone a good distance ahead. They soon found fresh Indian sign, and actually heard the Indians; but the latter fled in panic. They came on a little Indian fishing village, just abandoned. The three low, oblong huts, of palm leaves, had each an entrance for a man on all fours, but no other opening. They were dark inside, doubtless as a protection against the swarms of biting flies. On a pole in this village an axe, a knife, and some strings of red beads were left, with the hope that the Indians would return, find the gifts, and realize that we were friendly. We saw further Indian sign on both sides of the river.

After about two hours and a half we came on a little river entering from the east. It was broad but shallow, and at the point of entrance rushed down, green and white, over a sharply inclined sheet of rock. It was a lovely sight and we halted to admire it. Then on we went, until, when we had covered about eight kilometres, we came on a stretch of rapids. The canoes ran them with about a third of the loads, the other loads being carried on the men's shoulders. At the foot of the rapids we camped, as there were several good canoe trees near, and we had decided to build two rather small canoes. After dark the stars came out; but in the deep forest the glory of the stars in the night of the sky, the serene radiance of the moon, the splendor of sunrise and sunset, are never seen as they are seen on the vast open plains.

The following day, the 19th, the men began work on the canoes. The ill-fated big canoe had been made of wood so hard that it was difficult to work, and so heavy that the chips sank like lead in the water. But these trees were araputangas, with wood which was easier to work, and which floated. Great buttresses, or flanges, jutted out from their trunks at the base, and they bore big hard nuts or fruits which stood erect at the ends of the branches. The first tree felled proved rotten, and moreover it was chopped so that it smashed a number of lesser trees into the kitchen, overthrowing everything, but not inflicting serious damage. Hardworking, willing, and tough though the *camaradas* were, they naturally did not have the skill of northern lumberjacks.

We hoped to finish the two canoes in three days. A space was cleared in the forest for our tents. Among the taller trees grew huge-leafed pacovas. We bathed and swam in the river, although in it we caught piranhas. Carregadores ants swarmed all around our camp. As many of the nearest of their holes as we could we stopped with fire; but at night some of them got into our tents and ate things we could ill spare. In the early morning a column of foraging ants appeared, and we drove them back, also with fire. When the sky was not overcast the sun was very hot, and we spread out everything to dry. There were many wonderful butterflies round about, but only a few birds. Yet in the early morning and late afternoon there was some attractive bird music in the woods. The two best performers were our old friend the false bellbird, with its series of ringing whistles, and a shy, attractive ant-thrush. The latter walked much on the ground, with dainty movements, curtseying and raising its tail; and in accent and sequence, although not in tone or time, its song resembled that of our white-throated sparrow.

It was three weeks since we had started down the River of Doubt. We had come along its winding course about 140 kilometres, with a descent of somewhere in the neighborhood of 124 metres. It had been slow progress. We could not tell what physical obstacles were ahead of us, nor whether the Indians would be actively hostile. But a river normally describes in its course a parabola, the steep descent being in the upper part; and we hoped that in the future we should not have to encounter so many and such difficult rapids as we had already encountered, and that therefore we would make better time—a hope destined to failure.

SOURCES

"Run for the Trees!" by Lamar Underwood originally appeared in *American Frontiersman* magazine, Athlon Media Group. Reprinted by permission.

"Churchill's Boer Wars Escape" by Winston Churchill is from his book *London to Ladysmith via Pretoria* (1900).

"Stalag Luft III: The Impossible Escape" by Robert Barr Smith and Laurence J. Yadon is from their book *The Greatest Escapes of World War II* (Lyons Press, 2017). Reprinted by permission.

"An Occurrence at Owl Creek Bridge" by Ambrose Bierce (1890).

"The Pit and the Pendulum" by Edgar Allan Poe was first published in 1842 in a literary annual.

"The Greatest Escape: A True American Civil War Adventure" by Douglas Miller is from the book of the same title published by Lyons Press in 2020. Reprinted by permission.

"Mountain Man Escape Epic" by Lamar Underwood originally appeared in *American Frontiersman* magazine, Athlon Media Group. Reprinted by permission.

"To Build a Fire" by Jack London is from his book *Lost Face* (1910).

"The Worst Journey in the World" by Apsley Cherry-Garrard is from the book of the same title (1922).

"Love of Life" by Jack London is from his book *Love of Life and Other Stories* (1907).

"An Adventure with a Dog and a Glacier" by John Muir is from his book *Travels in Alaska* (1915).

"The River of Doubt" by Theodore Roosevelt is from his book *Through the Brazilian Wilderness* (1914).